The Secret History ⅃ᴉᴉ𝗆pires

The
Secret History
of
Vampires

THEIR MULTIPLE FORMS
AND HIDDEN PURPOSES

CLAUDE LECOUTEUX

Translated by Jon E. Graham

Inner Traditions
Rochester, Vermont • Toronto, Canada

Inner Traditions
One Park Street
Rochester, Vermont 05767
www.InnerTraditions.com

Originally published in French under the title *Histoire des Vampires: Autopsie d'un mythe* by Éditions Imago

Library of Congress Cataloging-in-Publication Data

Lecouteux, Claude.
  [Histoire des vampires. English]
  The secret history of vampires : their multiple forms and hidden purposes / Claude Lecouteux ; translated by Jon E. Graham.
    p. cm.
  Includes bibliographical references (p.   ) and index.
  ISBN 978-1-59477-325-9 (pbk.)
  1. Vampires. I. Title.
  BF1556.L4313 2010
  398′.45—dc22

                                                                        2009042699

Printed and bound in the United States by Versa Press

10 9 8 7 6 5 4 3 2 1

Text design by Virginia Scott Bowman and layout by Priscilla Baker
This book was typeset in Garamond Premier Pro with Torino and Gill Sans used as display typefaces

Inner Traditions wishes to express its appreciation for assistance given by the government of France through the National Book Office of the Ministère de la Culture in the preparation of this translation.

Nous tenons à exprimer nos plus vifs remerciements au government de la France et le Ministère de la Culture, Centre National du Livre, pour leur concours dans la préparation de la traduction de cet ouvrage.

To Anneliese and Benoît

Contents

Introduction

From my grave to wander I am forc'd,
Still to seek the Good's long sever'd link,
Still to love the bridegroom I have lost,
And the life-blood of his heart to drink.
GOETHE, "THE BRIDE OF CORINTH" (1797)

THAT THE DEAD are capable of returning to afflict the living is a belief that goes back to the dawn of time: revenants are rarely motivated by good intentions. From this thought, the human imagination has conjured various forms that are little known to us, because, starting in the eighteenth century, they were all supplanted by a vampire whose image has gradually been crystallized by the famous Dracula immortalized by Bram Stoker (1847–1912) in a novel that has never gone out of print.* In fact this novel continues to serve as inspiration to other writers and filmmakers. In 1993 Fred Saberhagen and James V. Hart even adapted this story for the theater.

For a large part of the public, the vampire is a bloodsucker who comes to sleepers at night and brings about their slow deaths by siphoning away their vital substance. Novels and films have familiarized us with this person who allegedly dreads garlic and the cross, this living dead who fears the light of day. When the sun is shining, he remains in

---

*Two editions have been published in England (Oxford: 1983; London: 1993), three in France (1989, 1992, and 1993), and one in Belgium (1993).

his coffin or in a chest filled with earth from his grave. Here he sleeps with eyes wide open while rats defend him from any who might come near. A true living dead, the vampire has pale skin, overdeveloped and pointed canine teeth, vermilion lips, and long fingernails. His hand is icy cold and has a grip of steel. He leaves his haven to the accompaniment of ferociously howling dogs or wolves, and when he slips into a house, he causes the people watching over it to fall into inescapable torpor. Some assert that he can metamorphose into a fly, a rat, or a bat; that in this form he can spy upon the conversation of those pursuing him; and that he can communicate with his fellow vampires by telepathy. He can climb down the sheer walls of his castle like a lizard.

These details are based on long traditions that have come down from a remote past. Stoker put them together to produce what would become the myth of the vampire. He was inspired by earlier authors, but none had ever painted such a rich picture. William Polidori had shown the way with *The Vampyre, a Tale* in 1819.

Some great names have affixed their signatures to vampire stories, including Prosper Mérimée (1872) with *La guzla,* Charles Baudelaire, Lord Byron, Samuel Taylor Coleridge, Felix Dahn, Alexander Dumas, Hans Heinz Ewers, and Théophile Gautier.[1] The cinematic history of the vampire, meanwhile, began in 1913 with Robert Vignola's *The Vampire* and received its letters of nobility with W. Murnau's *Nosferatu: A Symphony of Horror* (1922), in which the victim holds back the monster until the arrival of dawn, which finally kills him. There were no less than seven vampire films in the period from 1930 to 1940—a rate of almost one a year! Since 1943 there has been an unending flood, and since 1958 everybody has had at least one opportunity to discover Christopher Lee playing the role of the vampire. Whether treated seriously or comically, as Roman Polanski did in 1967 with his *Fearless Vampire Killers,* this theme[2] of the vampire has enjoyed phenomenal success*—which clearly demonstrates that it touches a big question and a subject of great concern to people: What happens after death? First

---

*According to K. M. Schmidt, there have been more than six hundred fifty vampire movies since the beginning of cinema.

shown in movie theaters in 1992, all can now purchase a copy of Francis Ford Coppola's *Dracula* and shiver with fear in the comfort of their own homes. This was soon followed (in 1994) by Neil Jordan's adaptation of one of Anne Rice's bestselling novels about the vampire Lestat, *Interview with a Vampire.** The vein seems inexhaustible, and cinema has produced an abundance of excellent and terrible examples. In 1965 we witnessed the vampire integrated into the traditional Western (*Billy the Kid Meets Dracula*) and, in 1962, it melded with Roman history (*Hercules and the Vampires*). In 1961 it took the form of *Maciste versus the vampire.*[3] Who could think of denying the importance of this theme in the human imagination?

Sociologists explain the flourishing of vampire-themed literature and films as the combination of "meaningful" themes such as illness, death, sexuality, and religiosity. Furthermore, they have demonstrated that the vampire lends itself to political recuperation. Since 1741 the word *vampire* has taken on the meaning of "a tyrant sucking the life from his people," and Voltaire declared "the real vampires are the monks who eat at the expense of the kings and the people."[4] Karl Marx saw capitalists as bloodsuckers, and in 1970, in *Jonathan, les vampires ne meurent pas* (Jonathan, the Vampires Do Not Murder), Hans W. Geissendörfer identified Dracula with the triumphant Hitler—a way of saying that Nationalist Socialist ideas were as immortal as monstrous vampires—while Hans Heinz Ewers in *Vampire* (1921) merges the undead and the Jews. As Klaus M. Schmidt quite rightly notes: "By virtue of his nature, Dracula, the antichrist, possesses the power of inspiring infinite negative and positive associations."[5]

The success of vampires certainly resides in this power, and it is a quality that never fails: a rapid search of the Internet yields more than two hundred fifty home pages dedicated to them, with discussion forums and chat rooms!† The addresses are particularly delicious: "The Vampire Garden," "Vampire's Universe," "The Vampire's Lair,"

---

*Here the vampire is a rock 'n' roll idol who plunges his audience into a state of hysteria that comes to a bad ending.
†If you conduct your search using several search engines, this count will climb to more than several thousand sites!

"Vampire Mud," and so forth. We can note from an Internet search that there is a Transylvanian Society of Dracula, which publishes a bulletin called the *Internet Vampire Tribune Quarterly,* as well as vampire-themed nightclubs. In short, the fans of macabre curiosities are rather spoiled.

A terrifying figure because of its ungraspable qualities, the vampire has haunted the imaginal realm for centuries and excited the sagacity of scientists who have been seeking a satisfying explanation for his posthumous wanderings. As early as 1679, Philippe Rohr dedicated a dissertation to the dead that feed in their graves, a subject picked up anew by Otto in 1732 and again by Michaël Ranft in 1734. Ranft distinguished ties between vampirism and nightmares and believed it was all illusion prompted by a fertile imagination. Other scholars continued this endless argument: Gottlob Heinrich Vogt, Christoph Pohl, and an anonymous writer who signed his texts "the Weimar Doctor" devoted themselves to discussing the presumed nonputrefaction of vampires. This characteristic brought up a theological problem: theoretically, only the bodies of the excommunicated did not decompose. In 1733 Johann Christoph Harenberg did a complete turn around the matter, and in 1738 the Marquis Boyer d'Argens analyzed examples of vampirism.

Yet what gave substance to the belief in vampires and inspired a flood of scholarly treatises were reports from the authorities, such as those published in Belgrade in 1732 by Lieutenant Colonel Büttener and J. H. von Lindenfels on the vampires of the Serbian town of Medvegia* or the one published in Berlin that same year by the Prussian Royal Society of the Sciences. From these documents scholars drew information that they analyzed endlessly, and in 1746 Dom Augustin Calmet, a Benedictine monk of Senones, synthesized all the studies of this subject in his *Dissertation sur les apparitions des esprits et sur les vampires ou les revenants de Hongrie, de Moravie* (Dissertation on the Apparitions of Spirits and of Vampires or Revenants of Moravian Hungary) and so on, translated into German in 1751 and reprinted

---

*The translated record of the exhumation is provided in appendix 1.

many times since then.* For Calmet, vampirism was the consequence of the malnourished state of the Balkan peoples, which lent wings to their imagination. These rationalist and positivist explanations fueled the article Voltaire devoted to vampires in his *Philosophical Dictionary* around 1770. In short, added to the direct testimonies given us by local chronicles, there was an uninterrupted flood of information that inundated Europe from the beginning of the eighteenth century. To this flood we owe, in addition to those works already cited, several great literary works, such as "The Bride of Corinth" by Goethe.[6]

This huge mass of writing fed the contemporary imagination, but it also was the origin of errors and distortions suffered by the original belief, the origin of received notions and, most important, of the stupefying reduction of several types of wicked dead to the vampire alone. The books devoted to these bloodsuckers for decades have done little to restore them to their original appearance. They seem intended for the public at large—the same public that rushes to the theater in order to shiver with comfortable horror. These books have also given substance to the received notions with more or less good fortune, and rare are the objective studies that present the phenomenon and analyze it without falling into irrationality or without turning to the support of parapsychology or psychiatry.

My goal in this book's investigation is, through reliance on firsthand testimonies, to create a work of demystification, to rediscover the subject of an ancestral belief and uncover the mind-set in which the vampire is rooted. In my opinion, this anchoring in reality—even if this reality is no longer ours and we experience the greatest difficulty trying to plumb the motives of our ancestors' mind-set—is the most important factor if only because of its anthropological dimension. The vampire forms part of the misunderstood history of humanity. He possesses a role and a function—he did not just spring from nothingness in the seventeenth

---

*Calmet also influenced the nineteenth-century authors of popular novels—Ponson de Terrail, for example, who, in *La Baronne trépassée* (The Deceased Baroness, 1853) put these words in the mouth of his hero: "He was dealing with one of those monsters that are so well-known in Hungary and Bohemia, which they call vampires, about whom a monk, Father Dom Calmet, had recently, merely two or three years ago, written a very fine book specifically . . ."

or eighteenth century! He fits within a complex set of representations of life and death that has survived into the present, although clearly with a lesser richness than in the remote past—a past that people tend to confuse with the Dark Ages, those backward and ignorant times that were banished by reason and the Age of Enlightenment.

Yet it is startling that it was in the century of the Enlightenment that vampires spread like an epidemic into every region. Isn't this a curious fact? It seems that in the effort to enlighten minds, it was necessary to take up again, analyze, and dissect the ancient beliefs in order to display all their inanity. Of course! But the effect was only partial, and arguments convinced only those who were already persuaded that the ancient beliefs represented overheated senses, optical illusions, or a disordered imagination. Vampires, however, have never ceased fascinating the living, no doubt because they are "a rift in the framework of scientific certitudes so seamlessly woven that it seems they should never have to suffer the assault of the impossible," as Roger Caillois says.

Symbol of the intrusion of death and the beyond by sneaky and brutal paths in a universe that excludes them, the vampire represents the disquiet that is created from a rupture of order, a fissure, a discrepancy, or a contradiction. The serial writer Leon Gozlan expressed it well in 1861: "[B]ut vampires fit into no order, no class, or any reckoning of creation. They are neither death nor life, they are death taking on the appearance of life; or rather they are the terrifying grimace of one and the other. The dead reject the night with fear and the living dread it no less."[7] In short, they are pariahs, exiles, and we could almost bemoan their sorry fate. In fact, Paul Féval has someone say to Addhéma the vampire: "Kill me, kill me, I beg you in the name of the Father, the Son, and the Holy Ghost! My most terrible misery would be to live this death and die in this life."[8] In 1875, in *La Ville vampire* (The Vampire City), Féval defines these disturbing figures as a "prodigious people the wrath of God has attached to the surfaces of the earth, and whose sons, half demon, half ghost, both living and dead, are incapable of reproducing but are deprived as well of the benefit of dying."[9]

I must add a word about my sources. Leaving aside the eighteenth-century treatises that analyze vampire stories, I have gone back to the original texts that provided the content for these contemplations, and you will find some of them in the appendices. These are essentially extracts from local chronicles, newspapers, and what are mistakenly described as "legends." The so-called legends are in fact memorats—that is, the stories about an event deemed worthy to hand down to posterity because of its exceptional, disconcerting, disquieting, disturbing nature. This event either can serve as an example of the dangers the wicked dead can represent or can inform all of the remedies that will allow a community to react to a scourge and get rid of it. The legend is not a tale; the narrator accepts the past or present reality of the events mentioned, which, even if they smack of the supernatural, are well rooted in ordinary life.[10] The legend provides a permanent reference to an underlying belief system. With regard to the dead, this system is particularly rich because it has not yet vanished entirely; certain countries of central Europe are veritable conservatories of ancestral beliefs.

Because numerous studies have been devoted to Dracula, the incarnation of the modern myth, I here present all the individuals that have been gathered under the generic term *vampire* and restore them to the context of the mind-set of the time, thereby making in some way an archaeological study of the myth that the nineteenth century* forged following a long process of maturation whose steps we are going to revisit.[11] In this way you will discover an amazing world of which novels are only a pale reflection—even if they are fascinating by their addition of motives, psychology of the individual, tension, and an interpretation that is sometimes philosophical or religious.

---

*I deal here only with European vampires. In addition, there is the Hebrew Lilith, the Indian Pisâchas, and the Vedic Gandharvas.

1

The Vampire Myth

*When she had drained the marrow out of all my
   bones,
When I turned listlessly among my languid moans,
To give a kiss of love, no thing was with me but
A greasy leather flask that overflowed with pus!*

Charles Baudelaire,
"The Metamorphoses of the Vampire"

The Founding Writers

The founders of the modern myth of the vampire are three English authors: Dr. John William Polidori (1795–1821), J. Sheridan Le Fanu (1814–1873), and Bram Stoker. The first two are responsible to some extent for boosting the interest in vampires, but it was the third author, Bram Stoker, who literally set today's image of the vampire. The terrain was prepared by the Gothic novel literary movement initiated by Horace Walpole with *The Castle of Otranto* (1764), which brought back into style the landscape elements we also find in vampire stories: old castles falling into ruin, moldering chapels, abandoned cemeteries . . .

John William Polidori

In 1819, in *The Vampyre, a Tale,* Polidori painted a portrait of a disturbing creature who appeared at a winter party given in London: Lord Ruthven, an impassive gentleman with cold, gray eyes and a pale complexion, who seems to inspire anguish in even the most frivolous beings. He possesses a superhuman strength, and when he succumbs to gangrene, he asks that his body be carried to the top of a mountain so that it can be fully exposed to the moonlight. This is accomplished, but when others go to bury him, he has disappeared. He later reappears, causing the death of Aubrey, who has enough time to learn that Lord Ruthven, who had wed his sister, was a vampire, and the text ends with this sentence: "Lord Ruthven had disappeared, and Aubrey's sister had glutted the thirst of a VAMPYRE!" The ambience created by the author is fantastical, and he implies more things in order to excite the imagination than provides true descriptions that would allow readers to establish a vampire typology. Polidori's tale does not have a happy ending because Lord Ruthven is not slain and can therefore continue to suck the blood of his chosen victims.

We can also see this pessimism in *The Vampire of Val-de-Grâce* (1861) by Leon Gozlan in which people neglect to impale the vampire Brem Strombold, "an oversight that would cost them dearly. The *broucolaca** returned several times among the living and caused great woe in many families."[1] In *I Am Legend* (1954), a film by Tim Matheson, vampires have wiped out so much of humanity that only a handful of people remain.

Polidori's novella *The Vampyre, a Tale* launched the vampire genre in England. It was translated into French in 1819 and imitated by Charles Nodier one year later. In 1825 a new translation was published. Vampires enjoyed an unprecedented success. As a German critic correctly noted: "Polidori's Ruthven has become a kind of nineteenth-century Dracula." In 1820 the Theatre de la Porte Saint-Martin presented a melodrama, *Le Vampire,* as a result of the efforts of Charles Nodier, T. F. A. Carmouche, and A. de Jouffroy. This reaction was written in

---

*The dead body of an excommunicated person.

the Parisian press: "There is no Parisian theater that does not own its own vampire! At the Porte Saint-Martin there is *The Vampire,* at the vaudeville there is *The Vampiress,* and at the Variety Show there is *The Three Vampires or the Rays of the Moon.*" Bloodsuckers even invaded the opera. The most famous of these, with music composed by August Marschner and a libretto written by W. A. Wohlbrück, was performed in Leipzig for the first time in 1828.

John Sheridan Le Fanu

In 1872, with *Carmilla,* John Sheridan Le Fanu gave us a female vampire attracted to women,[2] which he placed in a long line of beliefs and traditions going back to the ghouls and empusae of classical antiquity. We can also find such a character in Théophile Gautier's *La Morte amoureuse* and in *The Family of the Vourdalak* by Alexei Tolstoy, cousin of the great author Leo Tolstoy. A woman named Carmilla appears one day at an isolated castle in Styria and reveals herself to be Mircalla, the Countess Karnstein, who has been dead for more than a century and whose tomb lies but a half league away. A series of deaths strike the young women of this region. Then Laura, the narrator, is attacked, and it is said that an *upyre* is haunting the forest. Sheridan Le Fanu scatters bits and pieces of information throughout his text: Carmilla, whose name is an anagram of Mircalla, refuses to reveal her family name, that of her domain, or that of the country from whence she comes; she never seems to eat; she does not say her prayers; she cannot tolerate funeral or religious songs; she leaves her room without opening the door or window; she is regularly stricken with languor; she has pointed canine teeth; and she takes the shape of a monstrous cat that brings to mind the painting by Füssli of the *nightmare** with whom the vampire shares so many features.[3] Here is how Laura describes Carmilla's first attack:

> I had a dream that night that was the beginning of a very strange agony. . . . I cannot call it a nightmare, for I was quite conscious of

---

*[According to *Merriam Webster's Collegiate Dictionary,* eleventh edition: "an evil spirit formerly thought to oppress people during sleep." —*Editor*] being asleep. But I was equally conscious of being in my room, and lying in bed, precisely as I actually was. I saw, or fancied I saw, the room and its furniture just as I had seen it last, except that it was very dark, and I saw something moving round the foot of the bed, which at first I could not accurately distinguish. But I soon saw that it was a sooty-black animal that resembled a monstrous cat. It appeared to me about four or five feet long for it measured fully the length of the hearthrug as it passed over it; and it continued to-ing and fro-ing with the lithe, sinister restlessness of a beast in a cage. I could not cry out, although as you may suppose, I was terrified. Its pace was growing faster, and the room rapidly darker and darker, and at length so dark that I could no longer see anything of it but its eyes. I felt it spring lightly on the bed. The two broad eyes approached my face, and suddenly I felt a stinging pain as if two large needles darted, an inch or two apart, deep into my breast. I waked with a scream. The room was lighted by the candle that burnt there all through the night, and I saw a female figure standing at the foot of the bed, a little at the right side. It was in a dark loose dress, and its hair was down and covered its shoulders. A block of stone could not have been more still. There was not the slightest stir of respiration. As I stared at it, the figure appeared to have changed its place, and was now nearer the door; then, close to it, the door opened, and it passed out.

When Carmilla sucks the blood from a person, she leaves a blue mark. At the moment when she is attacked by General Spielsdorf, whose daughter she has killed, she disappears into thin air: "I struck at her instantly with my sword; but I saw her standing near the door, unscathed. Horrified, I pursued, and struck again. She was gone; and my sword flew to shivers against the door." On a second occasion, the general strikes Carmilla with an ax "with all his force, but she dived under his blow, and unscathed, caught him in her tiny grasp by the wrist. He struggled for a moment to release his arm, but his hand opened, the axe fell to the ground, and the girl was gone." In order to rid themselves of this scourge, they open the tomb.

The next day the formal proceedings took place in the Chapel of Karnstein. The grave of the Countess Mircalla was opened; and the General and my father recognized each his perfidious and beautiful guest, in the face now disclosed to view. The features, though a hundred and fifty years had passed since her funeral, were tinted with the warmth of life. Her eyes were open; no cadaverous smell exhaled from the coffin. The two medical men, one officially present, the other on the part of the promoter of the inquiry, attested the marvelous fact that there was a faint but appreciable respiration, and a corresponding action of the heart. The limbs were perfectly flexible, the flesh elastic; and the leaden coffin floated with blood, in which to a depth of seven inches, the body lay immersed. Here then, were all the admitted signs and proofs of vampirism. The body, therefore, in accordance with the ancient practice, was raised, and a sharp stake driven through the heart of the vampire, who uttered a piercing shriek at the moment, in all respects such as might escape from a living person in the last agony. Then the head was struck off, and a torrent of blood flowed from the severed neck. The body and head were next placed on a pile of wood, and reduced to ashes, which were thrown upon the river and borne away, and that territory has never since been plagued by the visits of a vampire.

Sheridan Le Fanu knew his classics quite well, and the whole of his short novel is nourished by the reports of barbers, surgeons, scholars, and writers of the eighteenth century. The description above supplies the proof, the original will be provided later. Contrary to the claim of some, Sheridan Le Fanu had read not only Dom Calvert's book, which offered a summary of vampire knowledge in 1759, but also documents that lent their support to his writing, hence the scope of his text contains a kind of appendix reinforcing the reader's disquiet and anxiety.

How they escape from their graves and return to them for certain hours every day, without displacing the clay or leaving any trace of disturbance in the state of the coffin or the cerements, has always been admitted to be utterly inexplicable. . . . It is the nature of vampires to increase and multiply, but according to an ascertained and ghostly law. Assume, at starting, a territory perfectly free from that pest. How does it begin, and how does it multiply itself? I will tell you. A person, more or less wicked, puts an end to himself. A suicide, under certain circumstances, becomes a vampire. That specter visits living people in their slumbers; they die, and almost invariably, in the grave, develop into vampires.

Bram Stoker

The question raised at the beginning of the last extract is answered several years later by Bram Stoker in *Dracula*. The infatuation for vampires explains the genesis of this novel in which vampirological knowledge is theorized. Stoker created the character of Dr. Abraham van Helsing, the vampirologist, based on the model provided by Professor Armin Vambery of the University of Budapest, a renowned expert on the East, whom Stoker had met in London in 1890. Van Helsing informed his friends on everything they should know about vampires, and this speech is the veritable foundation of the modern myth:

> The vampire live on, and cannot die by mere passing of the time, he can flourish when that he can fatten on the blood of the living. Even more, we have seen amongst us that he can even grow younger, that his vital faculties grow strenuous, and seem as though they refresh themselves when his special pabulum is plenty. But he cannot flourish without this diet, he eat not as others. Even friend Jonathan, who lived with him for weeks, did never see him eat, never! He throws no shadow, he make in the mirror no reflect, as again Jonathan observe. He has the strength of many of his hand, witness again Jonathan when he shut the door against the wolves, and when he help him from the diligence too. He can transform himself to wolf, as we gather from the ship arrival in Whitby, when he tear open the dog, he can be as bat. . . . He can come in mist, which he creates. . . . He come on moonlight rays as elemental dust, as again Jonathan saw those sisters in the castle

of Dracula. He become so small, we ourselves saw Miss Lucy, ere she was at peace, slip through a hairbreadth space at the tomb door. He can, when once he find his way, come out from anything or into anything, no matter how close it be bound or even fused up with fire, solder you call it. He can see in the dark, no small power this, in a world, which is one half shut from the light. Ah, but hear me through. He can do all these things, yet he is not free. Nay, he is even more prisoner than the slave of the galley, than the madman in his cell. He cannot go where he lists, he who is not of nature has yet to obey some of nature's laws, why we know not. He may not enter anywhere at the first, unless there be some one of the household who bid him to come, though afterwards he can come as he please. His power ceases, as does that of all evil things, at the coming of the day. Only at certain times can he have limited freedom. If he be not at the place whither he is bound, he can only change himself at noon or at exact sunrise or sunset. . . . Thus, whereas he can do as he will within his limit, when he have his earth-home, his coffin-home, his hell-home, the place unhallowed, as we saw when he went to the grave of the suicide at Whitby, still at other time he can only change when the time come. It is said, too, that he can only pass running water at the slack or the flood of the tide. Then there are things which so afflict him that he has no power, as the garlic that we know of, and as for things sacred, as this symbol, my crucifix, that was amongst us even now when we resolve, to them he is nothing, but in their presence he take his place far off and silent with respect. There are others, too, which I shall tell you of, lest in our seeking we may need them. The branch of wild rose on his coffin keep him that he move not from it, a sacred bullet fired into the coffin kill him so that he be true dead, and as for the stake through him, we know already of its peace, or the cut-off head that giveth rest.[4]

When Dr. van Helsing, whom some have nicknamed "the Victorian James Bond," attacks Lucy, who, bitten by Dracula, has transformed into a vampire following her death—one of the major "explanations" for vampirism—he explains to his friends what he intends to do: "I shall cut off her head and fill her mouth with garlic, and I shall drive a stake through her body."

Stoker introduces a new detail into the myth: garlic, whose popularity was immense. Researchers have claimed that this phylactery had a long history accompanying that of vampires, basing their assertion on a fragment of Titinus (second century BCE) in which he says garlic should be hung around the neck of children to protect them from "the black and stinking stirge." Nicknamed "poor man's mandrake" in the Middle Ages, garlic was considered especially effective against spells. Like all plants that had a strong odor, garlic brought demons to flight. Demons, as we all know, can slip into corpses in order to reanimate them. It was this notion that was decisive for the incorporation of garlic into the battle against revenants. It turned into something that drove away ghosts. In Romania, cloves of garlic were placed in the coffin, the mouth, the nose, and the ears of the dead person to prevent its transformation into a revenant (*strigoi*). To say that beliefs are hard to kill is simply stating the obvious if we take as reference an article that appeared January 10, 1973, in a German newspaper, the *Süddeutsche Zeitung*.

Demetrius Myiciura, a fifty-six year-old Polish man living in London, had a fear of vampires bordering on panic, and it brought about his own death. A medical expert noted that Myiciura had suffocated on a garlic clove he kept in his mouth at night. Large quantities of garlic, salt, and pepper found in his room were intended as protection against vampires.

Abraham van Helsing also knows that the smallest orifice in the grave, tiny as it may be, will allow the vampire to leave, so he proceeds in this way:

First he took from his bag a mass of what looked like thin, wafer-like biscuit, which was carefully rolled up in a white napkin. Next he took out a double handful of some whitish stuff, like dough or putty. He crumbled the wafer up fine and worked it into the mass between his hands. This he then took, and rolling it into thin strips, began to lay them into the crevices between the door and its setting in the tomb.

When Lucy returns from her nocturnal wanderings, she is confronted by van Helsing and his friends as she seeks to get back into her tomb.

When within a foot or two of the door, however, she stopped, as if arrested by some irresistible force. Then she turned, and her face was shown in the clear burst of moonlight and by the lamp, which had now no quiver from [v]an Helsing's nerves. . . . And so for full half a minute, which seemed an eternity, she remained between the lifted crucifix and the sacred closing of her means of entry. . . . We could hear the click of the closing lantern as van Helsing held it down. Coming close to the tomb, he began to remove from the chinks some of the sacred emblem, which he had placed there. We all looked on with horrified amazement as we saw, when he stood back, the woman, with a corporeal body as real at that moment as our own, pass through the interstice where scarce a knife blade could have gone.

Another explanation was put forward during the Middle Ages. At the end of the twelfth century, William of Newburgh, recounting the wicked deeds of a revenant at Melrose Abbey, indicates that this undead individual, once wounded by the blow of an ax, "let out a plaintive and loud groan and turning round as suddenly as it had come while the stupefied monk hastened in pursuit of the fugitive, made its way back to his tomb. The tomb opened up for its resident protecting him from his assailant and then closed back up with the same facility."[5] We should note that this explanation is unique for its kind; ordinarily, graves are not endowed with properties such as this!

Alexei Tolstoy

Among the founders of the modern myth, we must also cite Count Alexei Tolstoy (1817–1875). In *The Family of the Vourdalak* he retraces the transformation of a family into vampires. Everything starts when Gorcha, the father, leaves with the other villagers in pursuit of a Turkish brigand. "Wait for me patiently for ten days and if I do not return on the tenth, arrange for a funeral Mass to be said—for by then, I will have been killed." But old Gorcha had added, looking very serious indeed:

> If, may God protect you, I should return after the ten days have passed, do not under any circumstances let me come in. I command you, if this should happen, to forget that I was once your father and to pierce me through the heart with an aspen stake, whatever I might say or do, for then I would no longer be human, I would be a cursed vourdalak, come to suck your blood.

His wishes are not respected, and he attacks and kills his grandson, and this is how a line of vampires is born.

> The child returned one night and knocked on the door, crying that he was cold and wanted to come home. His foolish mother, although she had been present herself at his burial, did not have the strength of mind to send him back to the cemetery, so she opened the door. He threw himself at her throat and sucked away her life's blood. After she had been buried, she in turn rose from the grave to suck the blood of her second son, then the blood of her husband, then the blood of her brother-in-law. They all went the same way.

Tolstoy seeds the text with clues that are the constituent elements of the myth of the vampire: when the monster approaches, victims are paralyzed; other authors speak of a great languor; everything transpires as if these monsters possess a hypnotic power; people avoid calling by name the individual suspected of vampirism or designating him indirectly, because this would serve to summon him from his grave; vampirism is contagious; vampires cannot tolerate holy relics (medallions, crosses, etc.).

From the Vampire
to the Vamp

Sheridan Le Fanu with Carmilla, Bram Stoker with Lucy, and Théophile Gautier with Clairmonde, the female vampire from *La morte amoureuse* (The Dead Lover)[6]—to mention but a few authors and women—created the character of the female vampire, she who would give birth, *cum grano salis,* to the modern vamp that the eleventh edition of the *Merriam Webster's Collegiate Dictionary* defines this way: "A woman who uses her charm or wiles to seduce and exploit men." Women vampires are irresistibly seductive, and dying with their kisses is a pleasure. This brings to mind the 1960 film by Roger Vadim, *Et mourir de plaisir* (Blood and Roses), a terrifying ambiguity that has contributed to the success of the novels that gave birth to it. Possessors of a cold beauty that demands complete, voluptuous surrender, women vampires feast on the pain and slow agony of their victims. Carmilla kills Laura slowly in contrast with her other victims, and the feelings she allows to be seen are disquieting.[7] Lucy's mask veritably changes: "Then her eyes ranged over us. Lucy's eyes in form and color, but Lucy's eyes unclean and full of hell fire, instead of the pure, gentle orbs we knew. . . . As she looked, her eyes blazed with unholy light, and the face became wreathed with a voluptuous smile." She advances toward her husband, Arthur, "and with a languorous, voluptuous grace, said, 'Come to me, Arthur.'" It is impossible to resist the appeal of a woman vampire even if, as in the story by Tolstoy, the victim knows she is dead: "The strength with which I embraced Sdenka with my arms forced one of the points of the cross you just saw to pierce my chest," Mr. d'Urfe declares. "Looking up at Sdenka I saw for the first time that her features, though still beautiful, were those of a corpse; that her eyes did not see; and that her smile was the distorted grimace of a decaying skull. At the same time

I sensed in that room, the putrid smell of the charnel-house. The fearful truth was revealed to me in all its ugliness."

The hero of the story just barely escapes from the embrace of Sdenka-turned-vampire, while Gorcha waits behind the window, leaning on a bloody stake!

Sheridan Le Fanu accentuates the disquieting and erotic nature of Carmilla, who tells Laura: "'You are mine, you *shall* be mine, you and I are one forever. . . . Darling, darling,' she murmured, 'I live in you; and you would die for me, I love you so.'" Her victim is the prey of conflicting feelings: "I did feel, as she said, drawn towards her, but there was also something of repulsion. In this ambiguous feeling, however, the sense of attraction immensely prevailed. She interested and won me; she was so beautiful and so indescribably engaging."

When Théophile Gautier recounts how Clarimonde comes to join Romuald again after her death, he declares: "I confess to my shame that I had entirely forgotten the advice of the Abbe Séra-pion and the sacred office wherewith I had been invested. [The protagonist is a priest.] I had fallen without resistance, and at the first assault. I had not even made the least effort to repel the tempter. The fresh coolness of Clarimonde's skin penetrated my own, and I felt voluptuous tremors pass over my whole body." The seductive appeal of the female vampire is such that the person who falls in love with her is ready to sacrifice his own life so that she might live: Romuald cries out, "I would rather have opened myself the veins of my arm and said to her: 'Drink, and may my love infiltrate itself throughout thy body together with my blood!'" Yet, contrary to Bram Stoker's Lucy, in Théophile Gautier's book the woman prevails over the vampire.

This voluptuous unease installed itself in the narratives as a constant, and Ponson du Terrail puts these words in the mouth of one of his vampire's victims: "He saw, he heard the vampire who was breathing in fits and starts. He felt it lie on top of him, inhaling his blood with greedy intensity and, a strange thing! Despite the terror and pain he felt, he experienced a kind of indefinable voluptuousness and bitter bliss at this atrocious contact."[8]

Imagination and the Belief

Thanks to the authors cited here, the constituent elements of the myth were established little by little. The central theme of the bloodsucker was enriched with fantasy motifs, the plot almost always took place in the remotest regions of central and eastern Europe, the names for vampires are foreign words haloed by mystery—*upyre, vourdalak*—which we shall examine further.

In 1981 Paul Wilson gave new life to the genre with *The Keep* (translated into French as *La forteresse noire*).[9] The story tells how a troop of German soldiers is given the task of occupying an ancient Wallachian fortress overlooking the Dinu Pass, but the occupants meet horrible deaths one after the other. A Romanian scholar, Professor Cuza, succeeds in establishing communication with the vampire, who reveals himself to be Viscount Radu Molasar, who lived in the fifteenth century. Cuza asks him: "Are you of the undead?" to which the other responds: "Undead? Nosferatu? Moroiu? Perhaps." Now the value of this extremely well-plotted story is that it goes back to original sources, thus Radu Molasar is indifferent to all the defensive methods customarily implemented against vampires: the cross and garlic have no effect . . .

But let's keep moving! The creators of the modern myth did not start from whole cloth. All their art consisted of collecting and reassembling the preexisting information and turning it into a fantasy tale. This was less simple than we might think, because it necessitated providing logical answers—or at least those responding to the logic of the myth, which was capable of earning the adherence of or causing turmoil in the minds of the most diehard rationalists. It was necessary to create horror, which, according to Julia Kristeva, is "what disturbs identity, system, order. What does not respect borders, positions, rules? The in-between, the ambiguous, the composite."[10]

Paradoxically, the vampire prolongs its own life by taking the life of other creatures. It is a veritable curse, and vampires dread death. We need only look at Théophile Gautier's Clarimonde: her health deteriorates, she visibly pales and becomes increasingly cold until the moment she sucks the blood from a fairly deep gash Romuald gives himself when cutting a fruit. She "sprang upon my wound, which she commenced to suck with an air of unutterable pleasure," after which, she exclaims: "I shall not die! I shall not die! My life is thine, and all that is of me comes from thee. A few drops of thy rich and noble blood, more precious and more potent than all the elixirs of the earth, have given me back life."

In the modern myth, love holds a choice place, something that is easily understood if we contemplate the words that Louis Aragon, in *Le crève-coeur* (The Heartbreak), places in the mouth of a dead man:

> *We wander through empty dwellings*
> *Without chains, without white sheets, without moans,*
>   *without ideas*
> *Specters of high noon, revenants of the middle of the*
>   *day*
> *Ghosts of a life where people spoke of love . . .*

An explanation was required for why vampires did not decompose, why those who transgressed all the laws of nature, those who called to question the notions of life and death, come back. It was necessary to know from whence they came, and if the common answer was "from the grave," Théophile Gautier has more imagination, and Clarimonde instructs on this point.

But I come from afar off, very far off, and from a land whence no other has ever yet returned. There is neither sun nor moon in that land whence I come: all is but space and shadow; there is neither road nor pathway: no earth for the foot, no air for the wing; and nevertheless behold me here, for Love is stronger than Death and must conquer him in the end. Oh what sad faces and fearful things I have seen on my way hither! What difficulty my soul, returned to earth through the power of will alone, has had in finding its body and reinstating itself therein! What terrible efforts I had to make ere I could lift the ponderous slab with which they had covered me!

An eternity of myths! These words are reminiscent of those of a revenant who returned in around 1130 to ask suffrages of his family so that he might be redeemed: "'Alas for me,' said the voice, 'insofar as coming from faraway lands and through such dangers, I have suffered from storms, snow, and the cold! How many fires have I been burned in and how much bad weather have I had to tolerate coming here!'"[11] In both cases the soul has undertaken an impossible and terrifying journey.

An explanation was also necessary for the supernatural strength of vampires, their ability to travel through walls, and their taste for blood. It was necessary to discover means for expelling the horror of these living dead into the hinterland of dream, to offer reassurance after terrifying the reader. In gathering the scattered elements collected by the researchers and scholars of ancient times, Polidori, Sheridan Le Fanu, Tolstoy, and Gautier answered the majority of these questions—but by no means all. The appeal of their stories rests in large part on the zones of shadow they left behind. In order to dismantle the myth, to find again the bits and pieces that have been so beautifully combined, we must plunge into ancient times and learn about the beliefs of our remote ancestors for whom revenants were a multiple reality. Only then will we be able to appreciate all that the modern myth transports by way of archetypes, which, taken separately, have not always disappeared beneath the blows of science and reason.

The Contribution of the Encyclopedists

Literature was not the sole vector for transmission of the myth of vampires;[12] we must also take into account the syntheses offered by the dictionaries and encyclopedias. In his *Philosophical Dictionary*, Voltaire devoted a long exegesis to vampires, which was very critical and full of mordant irony. Here is one passage: "These vampires were corpses, who went out of their graves at night to suck the blood of the living, either at their throats or stomachs, after which they returned to their cemeteries. The persons so sucked waned, grew pale, and fell into consumption;

while the sucking corpses grew fat, got rosy, and enjoyed an excellent appetite."[13]

Voltaire attacks Dom Calmet, "the historian of vampires," and passes sentence on the authors who dealt with this subject, whom he accuses of propagating this "superstition." The Voltarian entry is partially false and partially incomplete. Reducing to the nocturnal hours the time when vampires are active is erroneous, as is saying that they suck blood from the stomach. We shall uncover all the gaps in this article over the course of this book's investigation. Collin de Plancy reuses the essential elements of the work of Dom Calmet in his *Dictionnaire infernal* (Diabolical Dictionary) and in this way contributed to spreading and giving credibility to the belief.[14]

Around 1900 Larousse's *Dictionnaire encylopédique* (Encyclopedic Dictionary) delivers a succinct but very precise account.

> Vampires play an important role in the superstition of a certain number of the peoples of central and northern Europe: German, Hungarian, Russian, etc. Under this name are designated the dead who leave their tombs, at night by preference, to torment the living, most often by sucking at their throats, other times by gripping their necks to the point of suffocation. Formerly a great number of mysterious deaths were attributed to vampires and they figure in many legends. The modern Greeks call them broucalacas.[15]

The author of this presentation knows that the vampire is not only a sucker of blood but also a strangler. Contrary to Voltaire, he seems to accept that the superstition comes from Greece, and he does not talk about ways to get rid of it. A systematic exploration of this kind of work would no doubt be very revealing of the evolution of the belief in vampires, but it would be tedious here. We shall have to content ourselves with the two previous examples.

Let's now explore the background mind-set of the belief in vampires. This will allow us to better grasp how the modern myth was constructed.

2

Man, Life, Death

His jaw cadaverous were besmear'd
With clotted carnage o'er and o'er.
And all his horrid whole appear'd
Distent and fill'd with human gore!

JOHN STAGG, "THE VAMPYRE" (1810)

EVER SINCE WE came into existence, humans have been haunted by major questions concerning our origin, our future, and our end. We have provided answers that crop up almost everywhere, regardless of people or era, and if they have superficially evolved by virtue of scientific progress, they still give structure to how we think, and they find a particular expression in our religions. The surprising unanimity of the contemplations—beyond all their variations—is that the problem of life and death is truly fundamental. What is not at all surprising, depending on the nature of the answers, is that humans are capable of knowing either despair or hope, finding a meaning in life, and making the acquaintance of the absurd.

When we tackle our conceptions of life and death from the perspective of the wicked dead, we are quick to learn that it is propped up by the notion of destiny. In fact, since classical antiquity, scholars have maintained that each man receives a fixed span of life at birth. This span is on average seventy to eighty years. Psalms in fact states: "The days of our years are threescore years and ten; and if by reason of strength they be fourscore years . . ." (Psalms 90:10), and Censorinus (verse 238) informs us that the Romans divided life into ten *hebdomada,* which give us the same life span.[1] Any anticipated interruption of this span could have harmful and dangerous consequences, not only for the individual concerned but also for others who were living. It was therefore necessary for an individual to live his life to the end in order to fulfill his destiny and respect the time allocated him by the gods. If he did not do this, the beyond would refuse him entrance, and "passing away" in the etymological sense of the term would not take place. In other words, there would be no passage to the other side—the other side of an invisible frontier that separates the dead from the living and imprisons them in a world much like our own, with dwellings and countries. This invisible world is full of shadows bathed in a half-light, and it can be terrifying, neutral, or happy. It can be atop a mountain or inside one, on an isle beyond the ocean, beneath the earth, or in some ill-defined elsewhere. Depending on the civilization, this beyond is known by different names: Sheol, Hades, Tartarus, hell. It can be in two or three parts, most often consisting of a heaven and a hell, and later a purgatory—but it can also be the tomb or tumulus, the temporary retreat of the deceased. These beliefs coexist, and folk beliefs regarding this world exist partially in opposition to mythologies and religions.

Death falls under the heading of what are called rites of passage. Arnold van Gennep finds three distinct moments in these rites: the rites of separation, such as the preparation of the body and the departure for the cemetery; the rites of marginality, such as vigils; and the rites of aggregation, such as the funeral feast, for example.[2] If one of these stages is not achieved, the death is bad and the deceased becomes a danger to all.

A Bad Death

A first principle, a veritable theorem, therefore exists here: any individual who has not lived out his or her life to its prescribed limit does not pass away but remains stuck between this life and the next. As a result of this notion, the bulk of all ghosts were made up of suicides;[3] people whose life had been cut short by the blade, the noose, water, or fire; and anyone else who died prematurely (*immaturi, aori*). We can add to this number those whose lives were cause for anxiety in their communities: all those who were called wizards or witches; men or women of bad character; those who displayed a particular physical trait or birth mark;[4] those who were born on certain days or at certain times of the year; those born with a caul or double dentition; those who followed certain trades (blacksmiths, loggers, shepherds); all those who did not melt into the mass of their contemporaries (the marginal, the sacrilegious, the jealous, those who were abused during their lives and felt a desire for revenge); those whose manner of dying was bizarre or whose inhumation was not performed in accordance with the rituals; those who had no graves (*insepulti*);[5] those who were buried without the sacraments or in a place that did not suit them or even next to a detested neighbor; and, finally, those whose funerary dress or shroud was inadequate. Then there are also those who left a task unfinished, children of tender years, a promise unkept, or a vow unfulfilled; and those whose passing was mourned too greatly: their shrouds were soaked with grievers' tears and they are unable to rest in peace. All these individuals are not joined to the community of the dead and sometimes become members of those wandering hordes that make up the Infernal Hunt.[6] Monsignor Pierre-Daniel Huet, bishop of Avranches, who died in 1721, noted the Greek legend: "[T]hose who after a wicked life have died in sin, appear in various locations with the same face they bore in life; they often sow disorder among the living, striking some and killing others. . . . They believe that these bodies are abandoned to the power of the demon who preserves and animates them, and makes use of them for the vexation of men."[7]

We can see at once that this adds up to a large number of people. There was an imperative to guarantee the dead all they would require in their life after death: a tomb, livestock, food, and familiar and ritual objects. In archaic civilizations the dead man was buried with slaves and his wife or concubine. Here is an example of the danger in store for those who die in a state of mortal sin:

> A moneylender was buried one day in a monastery. At night he would emerge from his grave howling and storming about the building, tormenting the monks by striking them with a club, and would be found the next morning in a field in front of the town. After he had been reburied several times, a holy man cast a spell to make him reveal why he would not leave the monks in peace, and he responded: "I am lost and shall never find peace because I caused trouble for the poor day and night with my usury. On the other hand, you monks can find rest if you cast my corpse out of your monastery." This was done and he no longer was an irritant to anyone.[8]

The only dead who are not dreaded are those who led lives that conformed to the moral and behavioral codes of their societies. Lifestyle therefore had an immense importance, because passing beyond at death depended upon it. We must make a distinction, then, between the bad death, the one evoked above, and the good death, the one called "a blessing of the gods," the one boasted of in the *Litany of the Saints: Libera nos a subitanea et improvisa morte.*

The Good Death

The good death was one that crowned a good and beautiful life. It was an accomplishment and a summit for which a person prepared his entire life, as poet Rainer Maria Rilke says. Posthumous destiny depended on it, because the dead formed a community close to that of the living. This is the fate that an individual had time to anticipate and prepare for with the help of those Christian booklets entitled *The Art of Dying Well* (*Ars moriendi*), which were so widespread during the fifteenth century. At a much earlier date, the Bible stated: "But the just man, if he be prevented with death, shall be in rest" (Book of Wisdom 4,7). This is the "normal" death, one corresponding to the norms that a given society sets in this area. Numerous traces of it can be found in the medieval romances. This is what the wizard Merlin tells King Uther Pendragon: "Know that all the honors men may acquire in this world are of less use than a good death. And if you have won all the goods of this world, and you have a bad death, you risk losing everything, whereas if you committed much wickedness during your life and you have a good death, then all will be forgiven you."[9]

The good death was a deliverance, because it enabled people to leave this vale of tears and attain true life—on condition, these booklets say, that you have put all your affairs, both spiritual and temporal, in order. He who has repented, confessed, and received the viaticum; has returned all goods unlawfully gained and righted all wrongs committed—he shall be transformed into a good ancestor at the end of the binding funeral rituals, rejoin the society of the dead that extends that of the living, and become a nourishing humus. There are numerous medieval stories that recount the return of a dead man who asks his kin or friends to make amends in his stead. We have, by way of example, the story of Guy de Moras, who begs Étienne to ask Anselm, his brother, to indemnify all those to whom he caused harm, but Anselm retorts: "What does my brother's soul matter to me? He enjoyed his property for as long as he lived. Why did he himself not make good the injustices he committed? It's his business! As for me, I have no desire to make penitence for his sins."[10]

The dead person who had tried out and chosen his burial place, the one who had renounced this world and its material goods, this is the one who would enjoy a good death because, and this is definitely the most important point, he would have managed to loose himself from the shackles that chained him to this life. In Théophile Gautier's book, Clarimonde comes back, compelled by the love she feels for Romuald. It is because of him that she does not truly "pass away." In Sheridan Le Fanu's text, it is the impossibility of abandoning the world that pushes Carmilla to prolong her own life by murder. Renunciation of this life has not taken place and, when he is not the mere toy of a malefic fate, the vampire is a dissatisfied being refusing to obey the law common to all that pushes every individual into the grave.

"Death does not surprise the wise: he is always read to leave," says Jean de La Fointaine. A good death was also dying in the arms of your loved ones, then resting in the company of your ancestors, colleagues, or friends* in a select spot in the cemetery, near the Calvary display, for example. In 1077 Simon de Crépy-en-Valois justified the relocation of his father's body with a charter: "I have had it placed, in the manner of the ancients (*more antiquorum*), next to the burial place of my mother, his wife, and our ancestors (*predecessorum nostrum*)."[11] There was nothing worse than being buried "in wild land," "in bad earth," or "afield" because the sepulchre in "blessed earth" was not always granted.[12] Readers will recall that the graves of vampires are often well concealed—that of Carmilla, for example, is in a ruined chapel, and in order to move his field of activity from the Carpathians to London, Dracula is obliged to bring with him the dirt from his tomb. To be laid to rest in the fields made you an unknown corpse, a stranger, and exposed you to the risk of being used by witches for their spells. In Russia, the necromancer opened the grave of these kinds of dead bodies, and a prescription recommended to him that "before reciting the spell, he must . . . remove the lid [of the coffin], arrange the shroud, and then pass a needle through it three times."[13] Said needle would then be used for the wicked spells he had in mind and would serve the incantation as its material support.

The good death was one that had been accompanied by consecrated rites, from the prescribed funeral toiletries to the return to the stone garden, one that was followed by a vigil or wake, a period of mourning, gestures—such as those vouched for still in recent times, including covering mirrors, stopping pendulums, announcing the death to domestic animals, taking a tile from the roof to enable the soul to fly away, and so forth—prayers, and a meal accompanied by donations to the poor. These rituals have inflexible rules that had to be followed to the letter, otherwise there was every reason to fear the dead man: he would return to claim his due.

---

*The recurring locutions are in *tumulo parentum suum*, or *suorum predecessorum, sub stillicido, ad sanctos*.

We should realize that, according to ancient beliefs, the soul remained close to the body for a certain number of days because psychostasia, the weighing of the soul, generally did not take place until the fortieth day following the decease. The time separating the death from the funeral services was particularly dangerous because the dead individual was still endowed with a form of life, which Théophile Gautier depicts splendidly. When Romuald finds Clarimonde dead and laid out on her bed, he watches over her and tells us:

> The night advanced, and feeling the moment of eternal separation approach, I could not deny myself the last sad sweet pleasure of imprinting a kiss upon the dead lips of her who had been my only love. . . . Oh, miracle! A faint breath mingled itself with my breath, and the mouth of Clarimonde responded to the passionate pressure of mine. Her eyes unclosed, and lighted up with something of their former brilliancy; she uttered a long sigh, and uncrossing her arms, passed them around my neck with a look of ineffable delight.

Numerous testimonies originating in both the Middle Ages and the modern era tell us of strange postmortem manifestations—dead people who speak, stand up, try to leave, change position, grab hold of an object—proof, if proof is required, that what the Christians call *soul* has not yet left behind its former body.[14]

If an animal leaped over the corpse, if a bird flew over it, if rain fell upon it, if the people carrying the body looked back (Bulgaria), there was a risk the dead individual would return as a vampire. In Serbia it was believed that if the dead body was buried at a spot where a falling star had landed, it would lure the living to it. With the help of these few examples, which it would be no task to multiply considerably, we can see that a good death is no easy thing and, most important, is something not all are given, something that can also be found in the distinction made by our ancestors between the pure dead and the impure dead.

The Pure Dead and the Impure Dead

Russia has left us important testimonies about the distinction our ancient ancestors made among the dead. In this country there were two categories of the dead: the pure (*cistyi*), those who went directly into the land of the ancestors, and the impure (*necistyi*) who were continuously contravening the boundary between this and the next life. This difference is based on the belief that succumbing to old age was equal to a good death (*svoja smert'*), whereas those who had not lived their entire allotted time would experience an evil death (*ne svoja smert'*) and would not be able to enter the otherworld. Men struck by an evil death—suicides, murder victims— those who had not lived the time allotted (*vek*) and to whom fate (*dolja*) did not supply the required amount of vital force, would make constant demands upon the living to fill this lack. The land itself refused them: In the Middle Ages their bodies were hurled into impure places (swamps or ravines) where they were then covered with branches to prevent animals from tearing them to pieces. Among the southern Slavs, people who killed themselves by falling from a swing were regarded as impure, and they were ordered to be buried without the performance of holy services. In Bulgaria, those who die unmarried even today belong in the category of impure dead, and because, having never married, they are still unrealized beings, it is believed that the otherworld refuses them. This is why rites of posthumous marriage were established with a living human being, a stone, or a tree, a practice that could be found almost everywhere in the Slavic world.[15]

In Dalmatia vampires were divided into two categories: those of the innocent, called *Denac,* and those of the guilty, called *Orko,* a word behind which we can find the root word that also provided the English and French word *ogre.* The Orko was a sinner, and we know of an entire repertory of transgressions whose consequence was transformation into a vampire: working on Sunday, smoking on a holy day, having sexual relations with one's grandmother, and so forth.

Starting in the Middle Ages, the excommunicated became part of these impure dead everywhere the Catholic and Orthodox church extended their authority. The preacher Gotschalk Hollen (1400–1481) gives us a splendid example in his sixty-second sermon.

> When I was studying in Siena, Italy, I saw the body exhumed of a woman who had been buried seventy years earlier and whose limbs as well as her hair were all still intact. She was propped up vertically against a wall, and the entire city gathered to look at her. In the middle of the night, the sacristan wanted to go to the church in order to light the lamps for Matins. When he left, this body followed him and shouted at him that it could not crumble into dust because it had been excommunicated. "Go to the apostolic nuncio so that he may do me the kindness of lifting this excommunication so my body will dissolve." The sacristan obeyed. The woman was reintegrated back into the bosom of the Church and her body sprinkled with holy water; it immediately crumbled into dust.[16]

Witches fell into this same category of the dead, and there are many testimonies concerning them. For example, in 1738, the Franciscan Franciscus Solanus Monschmidt raised the question: What should be done with these dead witches and wizards who have concluded a pact with the devil while still alive (*cum daemone fecerunt in vita expressum pactum*) for the purpose of being resuscitated after their deaths so that they may attract the cadavers of Christians and even innocent children buried near them in the cemetery, and so that they may walk about, causing terrible unease among men and persecuting them? Monschmidt condemned the way in which executioners and gravediggers plied their trade in this regard and recommended exorcisms instead.[17]

We should also recall that Empress Maria Teresa banned the execution of corpses in Austria Hungry in March 1755, which in no way, until quite recently, prevented people from resorting to the tried and tested means of decapitating and mutilating bodies that were exhumed. The sovereign issued this law following the report made by court physicians Johannes Gasser and Christian Vabst on the case of Rosina Polakin, whose corpse had been exhumed in Hermersdorf in 1755 because she was suspected of vampirism. The family of the deceased was obliged to pull the body out of the grave by means of a hook attached to a rope and then remove it from the cemetery through a hole made in the wall specifically for this purpose. After it was exhumed, the body was decapitated and cremated.[18]

If the impure dead were by chance buried, the earth prevented their bodies from decomposing—we will see plenty of examples—and they were condemned to wander the earth, taking their revenge on humans. Therefore, to prevent the wizard of recent demise from returning to pester the living, his feet would be bound with a rope made from the inner bark of the rowan tree. To stop delinquent cadavers, the tendons of their heels and the veins of their knees would be severed "in order they could no longer stand back up," then a stake made from aspen would be driven into the center of their chest so it would pierce through the heart.

Let's take a look at some "recent" examples. In 1901, in Lichtenau near Iena, the body of a vagabond was discovered and then placed in the fire station. The next morning it was found tied up, and young villagers admitted to having done so to banish from its mind any thought it might have of wandering. In 1913 an old woman died in Putzig Canton in Prussia. Death struck seven family members in a short time thereafter, and it was said that the deceased was unable to find rest and was drawing her kin to the grave. Feeling that his own health was declining, one of the dead woman's sons followed the advice he was given: he exhumed the body, decapitated it, and placed the head at the cadaver's feet, and, wonder of wonders, he declared shortly thereafter that he felt so much better! As for sinners, putrefaction would not do its work as long as they had not received absolution, but their bodies would crumble instantaneously into dust at the time they obtained it through the intervention of those close to them.

We should note in passing that even animals would transform into revenants, because they, too, possessed a soul that was said to remain on earth for six weeks following death. If the animal was unsatisfied, it could return to trouble the living. Moreover, doubt would always reign in the presence of a beast such as this, for it could be the incarnation of a dead person. Bram Stoker did not invent the animal forms taken by vampires; he merely took existing beliefs for his inspiration.

The stage is set! We now know the kind of threat that permanently weighs upon the living who rightfully dread the deceased and hope to find protection by multiplying the measures intended to make them understand that they are respected and will not be forgotten, but also to make them realize that they are dead and should become accustomed to their new status and let the living go about their business. The funeral gifts, the gestures accompanying the funeral rites, and the commemoration rites all testify to this and are targeted on making sure that the *de cujus,* the deceased, is happy with his lot, that he has no cause for complaint, and that he feels neither resentment nor a desire for vengeance. What remains is to clarify how the people of the past depicted the life of the dead and, of course, how a revenant could have the vocation of becoming, more precisely, a vampire.

3

The Life of the Dead

I will not die entirely.

HORACE

IT MAY SEEM surprising today to talk about the life of the dead. For some this is sheer nonsense, for others a myth, and for the spiritists it is a reality that knew its hour of glory in the nineteenth century, when Arthur Conan Doyle saw the ghost of his son and when Victor Hugo had a revelation of the beyond on the Isle of Guernsey on the night of March 31, 1856. For some it is a mystery to be targeted, and those who have attempted it have formed organizations and have published books with evocative titles such as *Life After Life*. Others, such as Bernard Weber, with his book *The Thanatonauts* (1994), have treated the explorations of death humorously. In ancient times no one doubted that the dead continued to live either in their tombs or beyond them. This idea was still widespread in eighteenth-century Europe, and even today is alive in the country of Wales.[1] Testimonies of diverse provenance prove it to us.

The Teaching of the Memorats

At the end of the twelfth century Walter Map (ca. 1135–1209) reports two particularly striking stories in his *De nugis curialium* (II, 13).

A knight of the ancient Britons had lost his wife and had long mourned after her death when he caught sight of her one night in a remote valley in the midst of a large gathering of women. He was astounded and frightened, believing that the woman he had buried had returned to life; he wondered if he could believe his eyes and asked himself if he was a plaything of fate. He made a firm decision to carry her off in order to find joy again with his wife, if what he was seeing was reality and he was not the victim of a ghost. So as not to accuse himself of pusillanimity by refraining from action, he carried her off and was filled with joy by living with her for many years with as much happiness as before and by living in the world as they did before. Many children and grandchildren he had of her, whose descendants are many today and who are all called the sons of the dead woman. This would be an incredible and miraculous anomaly of nature if certain traces of the truth did not exist.

This event struck Walter Map so deeply that he returned to it later, summarizing the text while adding some new details: "It was said that a knight had buried his truly deceased wife and that he found her again and snatched her out from a band of dancers; he was afterward presented by her with children and grandchildren, and their line exists to this day" (IV, 8).

That a dead woman was able to move about and dance was astonishing, but that she was able to resume ordinary life and procreate was stupefying to say the least. Therefore, Walter Map, in the presence of an inexplicable "reality," extricates himself with a classic artifice: "We must accepts God's works in their entirety. . . . His words exceed our questions and escape our discussions." We shall hold on to the motif of the dance; it will crop up again elsewhere.

Mythic thought has used this type of testimony to advance a simple explanation supported by pre-Christian notions. Those individuals who were thought dead and buried were in fact victims of mysterious beings designated as *elves*. These elves snatched a person into their own world and substituted a simulacrum for his or her body. Toward the middle of the thirteenth century, Thomas of Cantimpré echoed this explanation. Here he mentions not elves, but an undefined individual:

> In the well-known village of Guverthen in Brabant, a young man who wanted to wed a young woman asked her parents for her hand, but his suit was turned down. In the meantime the maiden was attacked by a high fever, went into a decline, and was considered dead. People mourned and the bells were rung to advise everyone to pray for the peace of her soul. While the young man was making his way between this village to another at dusk he heard the voice of a young woman lamenting near his route. He made a diligent search, going here and there, and finally found this young woman and asked her what she was doing there while her friends mourned her death. She answered: "See that man before me, who is leading me!" The response amazed him as he could see no one else there. With courage and boldness he took charge of the young woman and hid her in a house outside of the village.[2]

He manages to extort a promise from the father that he can wed the maiden if he brings her back and shows everyone that the body over which they are holding vigil is only a pseudocorpse. "The young man then raised the linen sheet with which the body had been covered and all saw a body composed of such substances, the likes of which they had never seen before." Thomas then reminds his readers that "those who have been witness to these simulacra of human bodies created by devils say that their matter resembles rotting wood covered with soft skin." For the clergy, this was a diabolical illusion, an explanation that during his era had every chance of winning adherents. In fact, though, it is not valid; otherwise he would have gone to the trouble to say from the start that an invisible devil was leading the young woman away.

Thanks to a Yorkshire tradition that Sir Walter Scott transcribed in his *Letters on Demonology and Witchcraft*,[3] we have a folk and mythical explanation for a similar series of events that took place in the small seaport town of North Berwick.

An industrious man, a weaver in the little town, was married to a beautiful woman, who, after bearing two or three children, was so unfortunate as to die during the birth of the fourth child. The child was saved, but the mother had expired in convulsions, and as she was much disfigured after death, it became an opinion among her gossips that, from some neglect of those who ought to have watched the sick woman, she must have been carried off by the elves, and this ghastly corpse substituted in the place of the body.

When the weaver begins contemplating remarriage, his first wife appears to him dressed in white—therefore like a ghost—and informs him that she is held captive by "the good neighbors," a euphemism commonly used to designate dwarves and elves, and tells him the means by which he can deliver her. Alas! The weaver dares not undertake this task, and, following the advice of his minister, he remarries. His departed wife remains a prisoner of Elfland, which was the name of the land of supernatural beings who kidnap human beings. This belief also crops up in Denmark in the memorats, but here Elfland is Ellehøj, "the hill of the elves."

Here, we have been introduced to the theme of being snatched into the otherworld, a mythical vision of the fact that the dead continue to live. Thus the reality of the beliefs is brought forcibly to our attention. As early as the fourteenth century, Jacques Fournier, head of the Inquisition in Pamiers (Ariège) from 1318 to 1325, was recording the interrogations of Cathar heretics in his register, a gold mine for material touching on folk beliefs concerning death. Emmanuel Le Roy Ladurie sums up this data: "The dead get cold. They seek to warm themselves at night in houses that have a large woodpile. They light a nocturnal flame in the hearths whose embers the living had covered that evening before retiring to bed. The dead do not eat but they do drink wine, and of the best quality."[4] In fact, if we consider the whole of our corpus, the dead carried on many of the same activities as the living. They attended religious services performed by dead priests; they danced in cemeteries; they continued to love their friends and family and to hate their enemies; they defended their property and strangled or gouged out the eyes of those who would profane their graves;[5] they came and went; they gave news of themselves through specialized intermediaries—*armiers** in the Ariège region or wizards elsewhere—and they even resumed their professional activities, such as the Breton baker who returns after his death to knead the bread and encourage the work of his wife and baker's boys until the members of the village community, whom he is making uneasy, put an end to his wandering ways.

> They went to the grave in which he had been buried, and when they exhumed the body they found it covered with mud up to his knees and thighs, just as they had seen him walking in the street. And, because he had kneaded [the bread] with the others, they saw that his arms were covered with dough. Having observed thus, they filled the grave back in, but he immediately appeared again as he had done before and caused many wrongs and harm to folk. In the end they decided to return him to his grave as before and break his thighs. This was done, *and he was never seen again.*"[6]

The Return of the Dead

Contrary to a generally accepted notion, the marginal individuals—we looked at them in chapter 2—are not the only ones to become horrible revenants that sow terror. Dom Calmet tells us:

> In Warsaw, a priest who had ordered a bridle made for his horse died before the saddler had finished it. As he was one of those that are called vampires in Poland, he emerged from his grave in the customary ecclesiastical burial dress, took his horse from the stable, mounted it, and before the eyes of all Warsaw went to the saddler's shop where he first found only the man's wife. Terrified, she called her husband who came, and when this priest asked him for the bridle, he responded:

---

*["Soul messengers." —*Trans.*]

"But you are dead, Father." To which the priest answered: "I'm going to show you how dead I am," and at the same time dealt him such a blow that the poor saddler died shortly thereafter; and the priest returned to his tomb.[7]

In 1736 Tharsander noted: "In Silesia, most specifically in the village of Hozeploz, it is said that the dead often come back after their death, eating and drinking with family members and even having sexual relations with their wives. When travelers cross through the village at the time they are emerging from their graves, they pursue them and knock them down upon their backs."[8]

In short, the departed were not always successful in breaking the bonds that connected them to their former life. Those close to them definitely knew this, and until the nineteenth century almost throughout the whole of Europe, on certain dates, people left food on the table and the lights illuminated, knowing full well that deceased ancestors would be visiting their former homes, coming in to warm themselves by the hearth, which is why the living took the precaution of turning over the pot stand so the dead would not burn themselves on it. Helvetian testimonies collected by Josef Müller a century later are particularly revealing about this belief.[9]

Among the southern Slavs, particularly in Polesia (Black Ruthenia or Black Russia), the spirit-lover (*dux-ljubovnik*)* was often a dead man who took the form of a vampire or a flying serpent. Numerous tales tell how a dead husband visited his wife at night. The mother of the wife heard her daughter whispering, embracing, and kissing someone at night, and when she looked, it was clearly her deceased son-in-law, only he had wooden shoes in the place of feet.[10] In Serbia the vampire could visit his wife at night without causing her any harm. He could have sexual relations with her from which a child may be born, but this child had no bones and would not live long. Evidence for this belief goes back to the eighteenth century. The typical motifs serving as a canvas for

---

*Other names include *zmej ljubovnik* and *letun letajusij zmej*.

these stories are these: a young woman has lost her husband; neighbors notice that she is visited by a fiery serpent at night or her parents hear her talking to someone in her room; she begins growing pale, becomes thinner, and starts withering away; her late husband brings her gifts that turn into sheep or horse droppings; the parents take steps to drive away the demon.

In Poland the *latawiec* seduced women with his piercing gaze, after which they languished and soon died. Among the Bulgarians the motif of a marriage between a young girl and a snake was an often-used metaphor for death, and some natives of Byelorussia [Belarus] state that the snake-lover sucked the blood from those he had chosen. In Romania the spirit-lover was called *zburator*. He generally resembled a large, thin, young man who possessed many of the same traits as the vampire. This demon slipped into houses at night through the chimney and came to those who were consumed by love. The traces of these nocturnal visits— bruises, marks of kisses, and so on, which were identical to those left by vampires—were visible the next day. The person who was tortured in this way fell ill, sank into profound melancholy or madness, and then died.

The departed did not like being replaced by others either and, since the thirteenth century, displayed terrible jealousy, uttering prohibitions and death threats if we can believe Gervais of Tilbury (ca. 1155–1234), who reports that Guillaume de Mostiers appeared to his widow and extorted a promise from her not to remarry. Several years later she was forced to get married again, and her late husband emerged after the wedding ceremony: "Immediately, before the eyes of this solemn assembly, the dead man, raising the mortar, crushed his wife's skull with it. All saw the mortar lifted into the air but none could know by whom it had been raised."[11] This little "news item" reveals, among other things, that a dead person could take action, something no one doubted, and that he was corporeal: a ghost cannot handle a mortar!

Other stories clearly show us that some of the measures mentioned by Dr. van Helsing for ridding themselves of Count Dracula once and for all were in fact ineffective in older eras. There was a certain Henry the Northman, who died in the bishopric of Treves during the thirteenth century. An evildoer, thief, adulterer, oath-breaker, and incest committer, he returned to haunt his daughter's house, but "neither the sign of the cross nor the sword could put him to flight. He was often struck by sword blows, but he was invulnerable." His appearances ended only when holy water that had been poured over a nail from the Holy Cross was then sprinkled over the house, the daughter, and Henry himself. It should be noted that the dead man had substance inasmuch as "when someone struck him it produced the same noise that is made when striking a soft bed."[12] This consistency was called "fantasy flesh" in the fourteenth century.

Folk traditions from after the Middle Ages told that the dead formed a community. They had their own inn—called Nobiskrug, east of the Rhine—where they spent the money that the living had placed in their graves or in their mouths when laying them to rest. They attended their own Mass, and woe to those who surprised them there! We possess a handful of testimonies, the oldest of which is credited to Gregory of Tours. Between 1063 and 1072, Pierre Damien tells how a living person attended one such service and how a deceased gossip there told her she had only a year left to live and should atone. In the twelfth century, the monk Gunnlaug Leifsson reports how an old woman entered a church at an inauspicious hour and was attacked by the dead who were buried there, and in 1516, another woman met a deceased friend at church who warned her to leave the premises before the consecration and to flee without looking back, else she would lose her life. She followed this advice, but the dead raced after her in pursuit, grabbing her cloak, which she let fall. The next morning, she saw that each grave held part of her garment, which had been rent to pieces.[13] Do not disturb the dead, for it is dangerous because they are rarely kind: this was the lesson of a good many texts. Yet if we look at these testimonies through a magnifying glass, we are struck by a glaring contradiction: Why would deceased Christians—good, practicing Christians—attack their fellow worshippers who have come to pray? Was this a way of marking their domain and clearly making it understood that no one should have relations with them? No one knows. To borrow the huge medieval loophole, "the ways of the Lord are impenetrable!"

The most substantial body of work tells us of the love that does not die with death. It essentially consists of beautiful ballads and poems, such as Gottfried Bürger's "Lenore," from which Bram Stoker borrowed a verse when he wrote: "The dead travel quickly."[14] In the Greek *Akritic Songs,** a mother demands of her dead son that he bring back her daughter Eudocia, who has married someone far away: "His mother's curse forced Constantine to leave his tomb, the gravestone became a horse, the earth a saddle, his beautiful blond locks a bridle, and the earthworm became Constantine."[15]

He finds his sister and takes her on his croup, but all along their way, the birds keep singing: "O God all powerful, you perform great miracles [you make] the living walk with the dead!" Eudocia becomes nervous and asks her brother: "I am scared of you, my brother, you smell of incense. . . . What has happened to your blond hair? Where is your thick mustache?"

Constantine comes up with an explanation each time that hides the fact that he is dead. Eudocia arrives at her mother's and learns that Constantine has been slain: "Mother and daughter tightly embrace and both expire together." The encounter with the dead is fatal.

Many of these beliefs and practices can be found in tales that have become more or less legendary. A girl guesses that her gallant suitor is a revenant. She attaches a spool of thread to his leg to see the grave to which he returns. Another, invited by a revenant to visit him in his tomb, extricates herself from her predicament by asking him to go in first and then flees toward home while he complies with her request. One revenant lures a young girl to the cemetery, where she sees him devour a dead man's hand and drink his blood. Another is rescued by her father, who sticks a pitchfork into the revenant. Another saves herself thanks to a ball of linen thread, but another sleeps at an inn with a revenant and is found torn to pieces. A dead man goes to the home of his recently remarried widow, bites her, and slays her new husband. An

---

*Named this because they deal with the life of Digenis Akritas.

old couple turns into revenants: She appears in the form of a fly that murders all those on whose faces she lands, and he takes on the likeness of a dog. He slays his own children and drinks their blood. One day, three *rédivives,* as they were once called under the belief that the dead were living again, go inside houses and collect in a pitcher the blood of their inhabitants. When a revenant entered a dwelling, he caused the inhabitants to lose consciousness by touching them with the hand of a dead man—what in superstitions is known as the "hand of glory."*
Revenants, especially murder victims and suicides, pursued young people. The husband would appear to his wife as long as she had not pulled off his boots or as long as she had not said that she would go to the wedding of his brother and her sister. It was said that some revenants had a kind disposition, but only when they were treated well.

Stories and songs deal with this population of the marchlands of the beyond. For example: A dead fiancée devours everyone at her wake until a soldier plunges a stake into her heart. This restores her to life and she marries the soldier. On the tomb of a girl intended to become a revenant, a flower is growing. A prince plucks it and puts it on his hat, and that night the dead one takes the shape of the maiden whom he married. A young man hides in a revenant's tomb and is forced to bring him back a cauldron full of money. The belief is recuperated and embellished with a happy ending—the terrifying element is therefore banished and exorcised.

Christianity and Folk Traditions

Two fifteenth-century documents are also worth citing, because, despite their Christian wrapping, they do not succeed in concealing this belief in the life of the dead:

> The husband of a young woman died in Siena. He was buried but several days later he appeared to his wife while she was alone in her

---

*The hand of a cadaver used for all manner of wicked spells.

room. He reassured her, they then spoke, embraced, and kissed, and she stayed with him the entire day in the room. The wife no longer seemed so sad about the death of her spouse. Her mother-in-law found this surprising and looked into the room through a hole in the wall, where she saw her daughter-in-law with her late son. Stupefied, she sent out someone to bring back a Dominican who carried the host beneath his frock. The devil that had taken possession of the body and kept it so fresh that it seemed to be alive immediately fled, and this body was now seen to be rotting and filled with worms. They had the tomb opened secretly, but found no corpse there. The cadaver was then buried secretly outside the town.

The possession of the cadaver by a demon or devil was the canonical explanation offered by the medieval church, which, when confronted by perplexing events, interpreted them in accordance with its dogma.[16] We also see that the revenant was none other than the man who was buried: when he wandered off on an adventure, his grave was empty.

The second testimony is just as revealing and shows that the ecclesiastics often remained completely disarmed in the presence of revenant phenomena.

An old fiddler was buried with his instrument. After his death, his grave opened at midnight, he came out, and he began playing a dance tune. Little men and women sprung out of the neighboring tombs and joined him, starting to dance. The night watchman saw this from the belfry and told others so that the next night, a number of the curious had gathered in the cemetery. The dead hurled themselves on the spectators; some of them fainted from fright and some of them lost their lives. The clergy vainly attempted to put an end to these hauntings that kept recurring. The dance of the dead was finally brought to an end once the advice of several universities had been heeded and the suspect bodies dug up. These corpses were then pierced with stakes made of black thorn and decapitated with a spade.[17]

It was from similar information that Goethe wrote in 1813 a ballad entitled "The Dance of Death" in which he combined a Bohemian legend with a German one. At night a warder witnesses the emergence of the dead from their graves. They throw off their white shirts and indulge themselves in a saraband that the author treats in a comic style. The skeletons make deranged movements, their bones clink and clank. . . . The warder snatches one of the shirts and regains his post, but when the dance is over, the dead man who does not find his shirt starts scaling the tower to take it back.

> *The warder shook, and the warder grew pale,*
> *And gladly the shroud would have yielded!*
> *The ghost had its clutch on the last iron tail*
> *Which the top of the watch-tower shielded.*
> *When the moon was obscured by the rush of a cloud,*
> *One! Thundered the bell, and unswathed by a shroud,*
> *Down went the skeleton crashing![18]*

Compare this poem with the text provided in appendix 2, which represents the "reality" as the people of the past experienced it.

It is beyond the shadow of a doubt that literature was the creator of this myth out of beliefs recorded in the memorats. Contrary to what is said in the Bible (Book of Wisdom 2, 5) and what was espoused by the medieval church,* the dead person did retrace his steps, and the affixed seal in no way prevents the dead from returning. Death was not a dreamless sleep at the bottom of a dark prison. Revenants were the proof of this.

How to Become a Vampire

The vampire falls under the heading of a specific family of revenants—but why does a person become a vampire and not simply a revenant?

---

*The Bible does mention necromancy (1 Samuel 28), which compels the dead to speak.

What do folk traditions have to tell us in this regard, and what is their contribution to the modern myth?

Writers often present vampirism as a curse resulting from a bite—or else, the cause remains unexplained, which contributes even more to the reader's instability and the creation of a fantasy ambience. Folk beliefs have advanced quite a few other explanations, particularly in eastern and southern Europe, the true conservatory of revenants that has gradually been regarded as the cradle of these monsters. The time of death is particularly dangerous, we are told, because the fate of the dead person is sometimes at stake at this time. You may judge this in the following summary:

Citizen Johannes Cuntze, an inhabitant of Bendschin near Jägendorf and a man esteemed by all, was struck by a horse and was on his deathbed. Because of unconfessed misdeeds, he despaired of divine mercy. His son, who was watching over him at night, saw at around three o'clock a cat that opened the window and jumped onto the face of the dying man, as if he wanted to carry it off, then it left again. Death befell the man that next instant. Not a word was said about Cuntze's terrible end and the body was interred in the church, near the altar. At the time of his death and during the interment it rained heavily. Three days later a ghost resembling the deceased appeared, which tormented sleepers in their beds and animals in their stables. This phenomenon recurred: the ghost jumped people and strangled them in such a way that the marks it left remained visible for a long time, he crushed women in labor, and snatched children from their cradles. The common folk, believing that mouse holes were ever to be found in the tombs of wizards, examined Cuntze's resting place and found one. Although they plugged it up, it was gaping wide open again the next day. Spots of blood even appeared on the altar cloth. The ghost sucked the milk of cattle. Eventually the man was disinterred: his cadaver was still intact with a freshly grown new skin. His eyes were sometimes open and sometimes closed, and his head was turned toward the north the first day and toward the south on the second. When the corpse was injured, fresh blood flowed out although the dead man had been resting in the ground from February 8 to July 20. The body was placed in a bonfire but the executioner had to keep relighting it all day for the corpse to be totally reduced to ash. These ashes were then cast into the river.[19]

This explains how the intervention of an apparently malefic or diabolical cat suffices to transform Johannes Cuntze into a vampire. It is curious to see that in Romanian beliefs this animal bore no love for its masters and desired their death so it alone could reign over the house, and when a family member died, the cat was ejected from the house so that it could not eat the corpse's nose or walk beneath the coffin, which would transform the dead person into a revenant. The effusion of fresh blood and the movements of the eyes and head betrayed the truth of his new state. Several details are worth singling out: Being buried within a church prevented nothing. The manifestations of the dead man led people to the conclusion that he was a wizard, which was confirmed by his sucking the milk of cattle. In fact, one of the names of these wicked creatures in olden times was "milk thief."* Finally, the dead man behaved like a nightmare. We should note that the inhabitants of Bendschin had a reading grid at their disposal and an appreciation of events and knew the modalities for the elimination of this scourge. In Bulgaria any cadaver under which walked a chicken or a cat or any dying person who had not received the oil of extreme unction would transform into a vampire.

In Romania the origin of the strigoï is explained in this way: they were dead people over or under whose bodies an animal had crossed or people born with a caul or who had swallowed their amniotic membrane. In this latter case the midwife had to remove the membrane immediately and bury it or burn it and force the newborn to ingest its ashes, or she had to climb to the rooftop and reveal that a future revenant had just been born. They might also have been those who

---

*Generally in the feminine, *Milchdieberin* in German. We should not forget that the German *Alp* suckles men, women's breasts, and cows' udders. The *Drude* does the same.

had begun suckling upon their mother after being weaned* or those who cried within their mother's body. Perhaps they were the children of witches, illegitimate children whose mothers had killed them or left them to die of exposure before baptism, children resulting from incest, the progeny of witches and murderers, the seventh child of a family, or changelings—that is, children replaced by those of demons or other supernatural beings. They could also be those who were born with a tail, a sign of their vampiric predestination—but they could be saved if the tail was cut off with a small piece of money. Finally, there was the man who, during his lifetime, signed a pact with the devil. The connection with sorcery was extremely frequent in folk beliefs.

In addition to these well-defined future vampires, we find potential vampires. These included redheads, brothers who came into the world during the same month, individuals who were werewolves during their lifetime, evildoers, oath breakers, hanged men, those who never ate garlic, those who had the evil eye, those sworn to the devil's service, and those buried at sunset. Latvian folk songs (*dainas*) offer valuable information here: if you wish the dead to make their way into the beyond, they must be buried before noon, the hour that marks the beginning of the sun's decline and opens the way to sunset.

> *Bury me before noon,*
> *After noon do not bury me,*
> *After noon the Children of God*
> *Have closed the gates of Heaven.*[20]

Those buried after noon killed their relatives. They made their way into houses through the chimney, where they tortured, disfigured, strangled, or suffocated people. They ate the hearts of animals and humans; sucked their blood; demanded food, drink, and clothing; and they asked that their voices not change so they could hail each person by name. Furthermore, they had the ability to change into cats, dogs, swine, goats, other animals (but not sheep or cattle), insects, flames, light, and shadow.

*East of the Rhine they are called *Doppelsauger.*

They vanished, however, when the cock crowed, when the wooden clapperboards* echoed in the sky. It was believed that wild animals and evil spirits were revenants. According to Raymond McNally and Radu Florescu: "Who can become a vampire? In Transylvania, criminals, bastards, witches, magicians, excommunicated people, those born with teeth or a caul, and unbaptized children can all become vampires. The seventh son of a seventh son is doomed to become a vampire."[21]

Almost throughout all Europe (not only Transylvania), it was believed that if several boys were born in a row, the fifth or the seventh child would become a vampire. In fifteenth-century Picardy, they transformed into nightmares or werewolves, which was one more demonstration of just how tight the bonds were between these different creatures. The folk possessing two hearts and two souls, the *dvoeduschniki* of the Slavs, made excellent vampires because one of their souls—what is called the "outer soul, the *alter ego*"[22]—was able to leave the body for a time and cause harm to other people. This kind of vampire hid his "soul" beneath a stone and could not die unless it was found. Among the Kaschubs, a Wende people of Pomerania, a child born with a caul on a Saturday or during the Christmas holidays would be afflicted by this curse. Here is how a local journalist synthesized the information on vampires around 1820:

> In the Kaschub region, it happens at times that children are born with a very fine caul that resembles a small bonnet. If you wish to avoid that child transforming into a vampire after his death, you must take that caul, dry it, and preserve it carefully. Before the mother visits the church for the *relevailles* [benediction of the mother shortly after giving birth] and making her offering there, she should burn the caul, pulverize the ashes into a powder, and than have the child ingest it mixed with her milk. If this is not done and the child born with a caul dies before swallowing it in this manner, a terrible misfortune ensues. Once he has been buried, he will rise again from his coffin, start by

---

*These small boards were used during the Orthodox service as a signal addressed to the faithful. In the medieval West, they were used in the monasteries. See *Ecclesiastica offica* 94, 2.

devouring all the flesh of his hands and feet, including the shroud, then leave his sepulchre to go eat the living. First his closet and most distant relatives, then, once they are all dead, he will ring the bell of the village church and everyone should die that hears it, both young and old. Against these devourers there exists only one means: exhume them and separate their heads from their bodies with a spade.[23]

It was also said in Poland that the *strzygi* climbed up to the top of the church steeple at night and that all who were his age would die as far as he can see. The fact that a vampire was at work would be revealed when people within a certain vicinity were suddenly struck by an unknown illness. Victims went into a languor, started wasting away, and soon died. Vampirologists who examined these maladies proceeded as modern doctors do and questioned their patients, whose statements confirmed what the vampirologists had been able to deduce.

In *Carmilla,* Le Fanu shows the vampire's victims stricken by nightmares then "lastly came sensations. One, not unpleasant, but very peculiar, she said, resembled the flow of an icy stream against her breast. At a later time, she felt something like a pair of large needles piercing her, a little below the throat, with a very sharp pain. A few nights after, followed a gradual and convulsive strangulation." Another victim, for her part, states:

> Sometimes it was as if warm lips kissed me, and longer and longer and more lovingly as they reached my throat, but there the caress fixed itself. My heart beat faster, my breathing rose and fell rapidly and full drawn; a sobbing, that rose into a sense of strangulation, supervened and turned into a dreadful convulsion, in which my senses left me and I became unconscious.

When the "specialist" examines his patient's throat, he discovers "a small blue spot, about the size of the tip of your little finger." There is no longer any possible doubt: she has been bitten by a vampire. Everyone knows that, according to modern myth, this bite is going to determine the transition to the state of vampire.

4

Precursors of the Vampire

The Night-Mare Life-In-Death was she,
Who thicks man's blood with cold. . . .
Fear at my heart, as at a cup,
My lifeblood seemed to sip . . .

SAMUEL TAYLOR COLERIDGE,
"THE RIME OF THE ANCIENT MARINER"

AS WE HAVE SEEN, the character of the vampire has been formed from preexisting elements, so it would be very helpful to become acquainted with these. For our purposes, I have provided a name for each of the revenants that have bequeathed a feature of their character to the vampire, and, in order to do this, I have taken inspiration from either their characteristic actions or the folk names by which they are known in other languages.

The Summoner

While vampires bring death to the living by drinking their blood, there are quite a few other ways to kill. We can detect these in the prehistory of these harmful dead. The first and one of the oldest is what we could call the *summoning*, a technical term borrowed from magic, where it serves to designate the conjuring of a supernatural being: a dead person appearing in flesh and bone—because these revenants are always corporeal, as we have seen in a previous study[1]—who calls the living by their name, which soon brings about their death.

Walter Map, a clerk attached to England's chancellery of King Henry II, then archdeacon at Oxford, was the first medieval author to relate the following, which he considered to be a miracle that took place between 1149 and 1182 in the country of Wales. The knight William Laudun came to Gilbert Foliot, bishop of Hereford, and told him:

> My Lord, I come to you for advice. A Welshman of evil life died of late unchristianly enough in my village and straightaway after four nights took to coming back every night to the village, and will not desist from summoning singly and by name his fellow-villagers, who upon being called at once fall sick and die within three days, so that now there are very few of them left.[2]

Let's single out a few details in this telling. The departed did not have an aura of saintliness, and his death conformed to his life: wicked he was, wicked he shall remain. He returns to kill his fellow villagers, and it is enough that he calls them by name. The bishop suggests a Christian explanation—it is a fallen angel who has slipped into the corpse, the theme of possession—and indicates what steps to take, a curious blend of pagan and Christian measures: "Let the body be exhumed, cut the neck through with a spade, and sprinkle the body and grave well with holy water, and replace it." These measures, however, have no effect whatsoever, because this revenant is particularly tough and continues dealing out death. Eventually, the villagers abandon their homes.

> So one night when the summoner had left but few alive, he called William himself, citing him thrice. He [William], however, bold and quick as he was, and awake to the situation, darted out with his sword drawn, and chased the demon, who fled up to the grave,

and there, as he fell into it, clave his head to the neck. From that moment the ravages of that wandering pestilence ceased and did no more hurt either to William or to anyone else.

We can note one contradiction in this text: decapitating the corpse has no effect at all but splitting it in half "kills" it once and for all. A detail such as this reveals that Walter Map drew his inspiration from a folktale, which remains indifferent to this kind of unlikelihood, unless the intention is to signify to us that the power of the sword—therefore of the lord—is greater than that of the spade. Another explanation is plausible: decapitating the dead man is useless if no one takes the precaution of placing the head at the body's feet in the grave in such a way that the corpse cannot grab it and put it back in its rightful place. Archaeology has in fact taught us that this kind of mutilation is accompanied by the removal of the head to a position by the feet of the corpse.

Let's leap forward several centuries and look at what Charles Ferdinand von Schertz reports around 1706 in his booklet entitled *Magia Posthuma*.[3] Examining phenomena that today would be called paranormal, he mentions "a shepherd from the village of Blow near the town of Cadan in Bohemia, who appeared on several occasions calling several individuals, who did not fail to die eight days later." In 1751 Dom Calmet cites a book by Leon Allatius that says: "On the Island of Chios, the inhabitants do not respond to the first voice that calls them for fear it may be a spirit or a revenant. But if they are called two times, it can never be a broucalaca: this is the name they give these specters. If someone responds the first time they are called, the specter disappears but the one it spoke to will inevitably die."[4]

In the present, the English word *fetch* describes this phenomenon.[5] This word designates the apparition of a living or dying individual,* or even a dead one, and is always understood to be a warning, a premonition. The fetch is also understood as the entity that comes to take the person who is on his or her deathbed. A slight slippage is noticeable

---

*This intersects with the notion of *wraith* that designates the individual's double, which escapes when death is imminent.

here, because, in all likelihood, a fetch serves as a "ferryman" to the dying individual and therefore has a positive character that carries us far from vampires.

The Knocker

Another way of killing the living is by knocking on their door, an action that has almost the same function as the summons. Even if testimonies are rare, no doubt because they have been confused with the activity of a poltergeist, they speak volumes and go far back in time. Here is one, drawn from the *Saga of the People of Floi,* written around 1300. The plot unfurls in southwestern Iceland some three centuries earlier:

> The weather was beautiful on Christmas Day and people spent the entire day outside. The second day, Thorgils and his men went to bed early; they were already asleep when Jostein and his companions noisily entered the hut. They went to bed. They had barely stretched out when someone knocked at the door. One of Jostein's men leaped up saying: "It is undoubtedly good news," went outside, was taken by madness, and died the next morning. The same thing happened the next night: a man went mad declaring he had seen and been attacked by the man who died the night before.[6]

Other Scandinavian texts depict a revenant knocking on the roof of a house to induce the inhabitants to leave, but contrary to the story of Jostein, this is not followed by more deaths because the hero strikes down the pest after a fierce combat. The only knocks we should consider are those delivered to a door. Recall what Dr. van Helsing says in Bram Stoker's novel: the vampire can enter a home only if he has been invited in.

An Icelandic tale collected in the nineteenth century recounts how a deacon of Mirka, in the Eyjafjörder, drowns while trying to cross a river.[7] He is laid to rest one week before Christmas. Yet on the eve of the Lord's Nativity, Gudrun, his wife,

. . . heard knocking at the door. Another woman, who was with her, went to the door but saw no one outside. Furthermore, it was neither light nor dark because the moon was going in and out of the clouds. When the woman came back inside saying she had not seen anyone, Gudrun said: "It must be for me and I am going to depart now, assuredly."

Outside she saw her husband's horse and a man she took to be her husband. She climbed up into the saddle and they rode off. The moon emerged from the clouds and the deacon said:

The moon glides,
Riding death,
See you not the white patch
On the nape of my neck,
*Garun, Garun?**

They reach the gate to the cemetery where the deacon ties his horse and Gudrun sees an open grave. Though terrified, she has the presence of mind to grab hold of the bell rope.

At that same moment, someone seized her from behind and it was lucky she had not had time to put both her arms in the sleeves of her coat because she had been punched so hard that the coat ripped at the shoulder seam at the height of the sleeve she had managed to get on. The last thing she saw of the deacon was him racing away with her torn coat back into the open grave while making the dirt fall back on top of him from all sides.

Gudrun returns home, but "that very night, the deacon came back and persecuted Gudrun. . . . For the next half-month, she could not be left alone and someone had to stay to watch over her every night."

---

*The deacon cannot pronounce his wife's name correctly because it includes the root word *gud:* "God."

The Vampire *by*
Philip Burne-Jones

John Sheridan Le Fanu,
author of Carmilla

Carmilla suffering from a vampire attack

Anne Rice, author of Interview with a Vampire

Below: The Nightmare *by Henry Fuseli*

Bram Stoker, author
of Dracula

Bram Stoker's
personal notes

Bran castle in
Romania, known
as Dracula's castle

The Premature
Burial *by Antoine
Wiertz*

Saint Vitalis being buried alive from Martyrs' Mirror

This vault made premature burial impossible because a person could live for hours in one of the compartments and the handwheels used to open the vault were located on the inside of the doors.

Actor Christopher Lee, who played Dracula in several horror films in the 1970s

Actor Bela Lugosi portrayed the infamous vampire in the 1931 film, Dracula.

Dom Augustin Calmet, Benedictine monk whose treatise in 1746 considers the possible existence of vampires

Vampires often take the form of a bat.

Goethe, author of "The Bride of Corinth"

In această casă a locuit
intre anii 1431–1435,
domnitorul Tării Românești
VLAD DRACUL,
fiul lui
Mircea cel Bătrin.

A plate marking the birthplace of Count Vlad Dracul (Vlad the Impaler), the historical character on whom the Dracula legends are based

Earliest know portrait of Vlad the Impaler (Vlad Dracul, prince of Wallachia)

Albert Decaris: Le Vampire transfixé

Vlad the Impaler dining in the presence of numerous impaled corpses

Le Vampire *lithograph by R. de Moraine*

Finally a wizard is called upon who forces the dead man back under the ground with his spells and then rolls a stone over the grave. Gudrun recovers, but "she was never the same as before." The text leaves no doubt as to the meaning of this knocking on the door: The dead person does not return in search of simply any individual. He comes in search of his wife, and the narrator emphasizes this detail because the deacon remains invisible to everyone else. Though Gudrun does not die, the experience does leave her scarred for life.

The broucalaca of southern Europe is a summoner and a knocker at the same time. He has a habit of pounding on the doors of houses and calling people by name. Whoever responds dies on the spot.[8] These wicked dead are a foreshadowing of the vampire.

Beliefs have a hardy life. Around 1900, students told Joseph Klapper of the following belief in Gleiwitz (Silesia): "When a person dies, the night following his burial, someone knocks at his door. You should not open the door because it is the dead man outside. If you open the door, he will carry off other family members to the grave."[9]

The Visitor

The visitor can be considered a variety of the knocker. The sole distinction between them is that it is not said whether the visitor knocks at the doors of the houses he visits. In the beginning of the eighteenth century, a dead man called a vampire sowed disorder in the Moravian village of Liebava, and the canon of Olomouc Cathedral was charged with investigating the matter in the company of a priest to whom we owe the following narrative.

> Proceedings were held, witnesses were heard, the ordinary rules of law were observed. The depositions of the witnesses stated that a certain notable inhabitant of Liebava had often bothered the living people of said place during the night, and that he had come out of the cemetery and gone into several houses during the last three or four years. These annoying visits had ceased because a Hungarian

stranger, passing through the village during the time of these rumors, boasted he could bring them to an end and get rid of the vampire. To satisfy his promise he climbed up into the steeple of the church and watched for the moment the vampire left his tomb, leaving around the grave the linens in which he had been buried when he went into the village to distress the inhabitants.

Having seen the vampire leave his grave, the Hungarian promptly descended from the steeple, snatched up the grave linens, and carried them with him back up into the tower. The vampire on return from his travels and not finding his linens, shouted loudly against the Hungarian who was beckoning to him from the top of the tower: if he wanted his linens back, come get them. The vampire began climbing the steeple, but the Hungarian knocked over the ladder and cut off his head with a spade. This was the end of this tragedy.[10]

This dead man was no vampire; he was only a simple revenant! In fact, it is never said if he caused more deaths, and not a single allusion is made to any bloodsucking activity. He is called a *vampire,* however, which is evidence that this word first was used to describe mere revenants before being applied to bloodsuckers. The author of this report is therefore interpreting a haunting in accordance with rumors that had been spreading in Europe for several decades and therefore contributed to establishing the myth. In fact, the Liebava revenant is close to the one that William Laudun, according to Walter Map, expedited *ad patres . . .*

We should examine closely the translations of central and eastern European documents made during an earlier time, for they are often "oriented," and Slavic terms designating revenants have been systematically rendered as *vampire.* I was even surprised to find that this is still happening today—for example, in the book that Boris Rybakov has devoted to the paganism of the ancient Slavs.[11] A true vampire is designated by more than simply piercing with a stake the body of a man who died violently or drowned! On the other hand, there are other "visitors" who are indeed vampires. The thirty-seventh letter from *Jewish Letters,* published in 1738, presents a vampire visitor, and we can note the differences from the preceding tale of Liebava:

In the beginning of September there died in the village of Kisilova, three leagues from Graditz [in Hungary], an old man who was sixty-two years of age. Three days after he had been buried he appeared in the night to his son and asked him for something to eat; the son having given him something, he ate and disappeared. The next day the son recounted to his neighbors what had happened. That night the father did not appear, but the following night he showed himself, and asked for something to eat. They know not whether the son gave him anything or not, but the next day he was found dead in his bed. On the same day five or six persons fell suddenly ill in the village, and died one after the other in a few days. The officer or bailiff of the place, when informed of what had happened, sent an account of it to the tribunal of Belgrade, which dispatched to the village two of these officers and an executioner to examine into this affair. The imperial officer from whom we have this account repaired thither from Graditz, to be witness of a circumstance, which he had so often heard spoken of.

They opened the graves of those who had been dead six weeks. When they came to that of the old man, they found him with his eyes open, having a fine color, with natural respiration, nevertheless motionless as the dead; whence they concluded that he was most evidently a vampire. The executioner drove a stake into his heart; they then raised a pyre and reduced the corpse to ashes. No mark of vampirism was found either on the corpse of the son, or on the others.[12]

These two narratives (of Liebava and Kisilova) have furnished a good part of the content of the modern myth. The first tale can be seen in Sheridan Le Fanu's *Carmilla,* and the second narrative—no doubt, combined with another testimony—was the inspiration for Alexei Tolstoy in *The Family of the Vourdalak.* This other testimony tells this: A soldier staying at the home of a Hungarian peasant sees a stranger sit down at the table, and this stranger frightens everyone in the household. His host dies the following day and the soldier asks who the visitor had been. He is told that it was his host's father, who had been dead and buried more than ten years ago. It was he who had sat down next to the son and had announced and caused his death. The soldier alerts his regiment, and the count of Cabreras sends a surgeon, an auditor, and other officers to the site. Once witnesses have been heard, the count has the corpse exhumed "and it was found to be like a man that had just died, with its blood like that of a living man." His head is cut off and then put back in the grave. In Tolstoy's book, the count of Cabreras is replaced by the Marquis d'Urfe, and old Gorcha comes back and sits down at the table with his family but refuses to eat, then that night attacks his grandson . . .

The Famished

In *The Vampyre,* John William Polidori tells of his hero Aubrey's encounter with a young Greek named Ianthe, who tells him about an event that caused her family great pain.

> Often as she told him the tale of the living vampyre, who had passed years amidst his friends, and dearest ties, forced every year, by feeding upon the life of a lovely female to prolong his existence for the ensuing months, his blood would run cold, whilst he attempted to laugh her out of such idle and horrible fantasies; but Ianthe cited to him the names of old men, who had at last detected one living among themselves, after several of their near relatives and children had been found marked with the stamp of the fiend's appetite.

This vampire has not yet become a specialist in sucking the blood of the living. These consuming monsters in fact have a long tradition.

As early as the year AD 217, Philostatus experienced a similar figure, the *empusa* unmasked by Apollonius of Tyana after she had almost managed to get around Menippus. Apollonius told Menippus: "[T]his fine bride is one of the empusas, that is to say of those beings whom the many regard as lamias and ghouls. These beings fall in love, and they are devoted to the delights of Aphrodite, but especially to the flesh of human beings, and they decoy with such delights those whom they mean to devour in their feasts." This immediately brings to mind Carmilla. Bespelled and summoned to speak by Apollonius, this famished being acknowledges "that she was an empusa, and was fattening up Menippus with pleasures before devouring his body, for it was her habit to feed upon young and beautiful bodies, because their blood is pure and strong."[13] An empusa, however, is not a dead thing but a demon. It is possible, though, that through successive retellings, vampires have assumed some of their attributes.

It was toward the eleventh century that the famished dead put in their first appearance. The Russian *Chronicle of Times Past* reports a strange event that took place in 1092, in the Ukranian village of Polotsk. While the different versions agree on the event, the one known as the Radziwill Draft includes a notation that has disappeared from the others (see italics in the following extract).

> In the year 6600—since the Creation!—something quite strange took place in Polotsk; something that would happen to us in our imagination. A loud noise was suddenly heard in the street, with devils galloping about there like human beings. If someone tried to leave his home, the devils would afflict him, invisibly, with a wound from which he died. No people dared leave their houses. Next these devils began appearing in the day on horses and there was no means to see them directly; people could still see the shoes of their steeds. Thus they distressed the people of Polotsk and the surrounding region and for that reason people say: "*The inhabitants of Polotsk are devoured by the dead.*"[14]

The text uses the word *nave* (*nekroi*) to designate what is killing the Polostkians. The scribes cannot decide to call them demons or the dead, but we can determine the second is the intention by relying on a philological item and the context. The word *nave* is relatively rare and apparently regarded as nonliterary; therefore, it may have been removed by the copyist of the Laurentine text that also uses an adverbial expression meaning "not in dream, but actually, openly." The event reported in the *Chronicle* would therefore have taken place in reality, not in the imagination, and revenants undoubtedly cause such a large loss of life. We should note in passing that these devouring dead form an Infernal Hunt[15] and arrive mounted on horses whose shoes alone are visible.

Another testimony, Scandinavian this time, passed down by Saxo the Grammarian's *Gesta Danorum* (at the beginning of the thirteenth century) and by the *Saga of Egil and Asmund the Beserker Slayer*,[16] is quite vivid in its description of the hunger of the dead. Asvit has succumbed to an illness and has been interred beneath a mound with his horse, his dog, and some food. Because he is Asvit's sworn brother, Asmund has been buried alive with him. A short while later, Asmund is pulled from the tumulus by grave robbers, and he tells them:

> I was forced to suffer a terrible ordeal because, regaining life, Asvit tore at me with his nails, fought with all his strength, and, returned from the kingdom of the dead, waged terrible battles after his death. . . . With his terrible teeth he devoured the horse and swallowed, what horror! the dog in his mouth. But his steed and dog did not suffice and he turned toward me with his sharp nails, slicing open my cheek and tearing off one of my ears. . . . But this horror was not long in receiving its just punishment; with a sure stroke, I sent his head flying and pierced his wicked body through with a stake.

Let's make sure to hold on to the pieces of information supplied by the last sentence, for we will continue to see them again and again. The decapitation is confirmed by archaeological finds, and the use of a stake to affix the revenant to its grave is well vouched for by ancient Scandinavian laws that have a precise phrase for this: "to bury beneath the stake" (*staursetja lik*). A passage from *Erik the Red's Saga* not only reflects the feat of the dead but also specifies an elementary precaution taken against them:

It had been common practice in Greenland, since Christianity had been adopted, to bury people in unconsecrated ground on the farms where they died. A pole was set up on the breast of each corpse until the priest came, then the pole was pulled out and consecrated water poured into the hole and a burial service performed, even though this was only done much later.[17]

This stake, which novelists and filmmakers have made famous the world over, was commonly used to fasten the dangerous dead—those whose deaths were suspect—to the ground, and around 1007, Burchard of Worms condemned the woman who, on the death of a nonbaptized infant, "carried its cadaver to a secret place and pierced its body with a rod. They declared that if they did not do this, the child would return and cause harm to many people." Burchard added: "If a woman does not manage to give birth to her child and dies in labor, then in the very grave itself the mother and the little one are pierced by a rod that nails them to the ground."[18] Standing in the background is the belief that mother and child can transform into wicked beings that will cause more deaths—that is, behave exactly like vampires before the fact or like those dead we are introducing.

Indirect testimonies show that it was believed that the dead could eat and devour. During the Middle Ages, murderers were identified by being tied limb to limb with their victim. If the person was truly guilty, the dead one would devour the living, and one case cites the case of a man whose mouth and nose were eaten by his victim.[19] The Greeks and Turks imagined that the broucalacas ate during the night and that the proof could be seen by disinterring them: their bodies were rosy and if opened, would let flow rivulets of fresh blood.

If we cast an eye over folktales, we see that they, too, knew the famished vampires and were strongly influenced by the historical data, which is to be expected, because these stories are found at the confluence of mythical and real elements. In a Gypsy story, a king notes that his provisions are mysteriously being eaten at night as his three sons stand guard. The first two see nothing, but the third spies a young woman who leaves her shroud and does a somersault. Immediately, her teeth turn into shovels and her nails into sickles and she starts devouring every bit of food she can find. In this story, the vampire has essentially retained its character as a devouring monster, but its food is not yet blood. Furthermore, numerous folk appellations for the vampire east of the Rhine have connotations of hunger and devouring. There is *Nachzehrer,* from the verb *zehren,* "to devour," and *Gierhals,* in which the root word *Gier* expresses greed. This term can be translated literally as "greedy mouth or jaw." And there is *Gierfrass,* from the verb *fressen,* "to eat like an animal."*

The Nonicide

The nonicide, *Neuntöter* in German, is a revenant whose wickedness is confined to causing the death of nine (*nonus*) people close to him. It is believed that he attracts those he liked particularly well or else, during his death, a mischance occurred: a cat had been allowed to pass over his body; his eyes had refused to shut; the head scarf of a woman laying out his body had brushed his lips, and so forth. Obviously, our ancestors explained his misdeeds in their own way by stating that this kind of dead man loved his family members so much that he wanted to keep them around him. The theme appears again in Sheridan Le Fanu's work without any mention of the bonds of kinship. Carmilla desires to have Laura for her companion in her life beyond the grave. "You shall be mine," she declares to her poor victim.

Perhaps the most ancient testimony on nonicide is a newspaper article dated July 31, 1725, that Michaël Ranft inserted in his treatise on *The Mastication of the Dead in Their Tombs.* This time the revenant is totally incorporated into a vampire.

> Ten weeks ago in the village of Kisolova in the Rahm district, a subject by the name of Peter Plogojovitz died and was buried according to the Raetz people's custom. It so happens that since that time the following occurred: in the village of Kisolova, nine persons, both elderly

---

*In Pomerania, we find *Gierrach, Gierhals, Begierg,* and *Unbegier.*

and young, after an illness that rapidly developed within twenty-four hours, died with an interval of only eight days, and while still lying alive on their deathbeds, they all testified that the said Plogojovitz (dead for ten weeks) had come while they were sleeping, had laid on top of them, and had seized them around the throat so hard that they were now going to surrender their souls. The villagers, keenly affected by this, had their fears strengthened yet further because the wife of Peter Plogojovitz, questioned by them, had admitted that her husband had come back to demand his boots in order to leave Kisolova and go to another village. It so happens that among such persons, that are also called *vampyri,* there are different signs of lack of any decomposition of the body. . . . Therefore all the inhabitants agreed to open the tomb of Peter Plogojovitz, in order to see if said signs were present. This is why they came to me [the imperial officer of the Gradiska district in Hungary] to bring me abreast of matters and to ask me if I would be able to assist at this visit by the orthodox priest. I answered them that such steps would first require the approval of the Administration and that I would take responsibility for their request, but they would have none of it. They gave me this peremptory response: I should do what I thought best and since I did not wish such a visit to be made without the permission of the authorities, they would be obliged to leave their houses because while awaiting Belgrade's consent, the entire village (as happened during the time of the Turks) ran the risk of being annihilated by the evil spirits.[20]

In short, the officer examines the body of Peter Plogojovitz with the Orthodox priest and notes: "Not without astonishment, I discovered a little fresh blood in his mouth, which, according to what I've heard said, would come from sucking the subjects slain by Peter Plogojovitz." Meanwhile, the villagers sharpen a stake and bury it in the heart of the corpse. "[T]hen they, in accordance with current custom, burned the body of this man mentioned so many times, an action for which I beg forgiveness if they made a mistake by committing it."

Peter Plogojovitz was simultaneously a nonicide, strangler, and vampire, which clearly shows that vampirism does not just mean sucking the blood of the living. It is strongly possible that in the folk beliefs the actions of the monster may have been focused on his role as a bloodsucker because of discoveries made during the exhumations, notably that of fresh blood in the grave, in the mouth, or gushing from the corpse when autopsied. We can also note that Plogojovitz is going to prompt the desertion of the village, exactly like the revenant whose head, according to Walter Map, William Laudun cleaves in two—and who also has the intention of performing his activity in a new location, which is why he needs his boots. This is the unique testimony of a traveling revenant. The fact that Peter lies on top of the sleepers establishes a link between the incubi of the Middle Ages and the nightmare, a recurrent trait of the modern myth in which, early on, the victim experiences great respiratory trouble before starting to waste away. Researchers have also noted that women are almost always visited by male vampires and men by female vampires.

The Appesart

Until the nineteenth century, a European belief spoke of a "spirit" that threw himself upon the people passing through certain places—cemeteries, crossroads, abandoned chapels, the forest, swamps. It perched on their backs and make them carry it a good distance, abandoning them only when they arrived home. This "spirit" was very often supposed to be a dead person, but there was no explanation for its actions. What can be gathered is that the *appesart's** victim remained in an extremely weakened state, as if a vampire had drained away all his vital substance and he was but a finger's breadth from death.

In all likelihood, the appesart is a pure product of the fear that invades a person when passing near what were formerly called "the uncertain places" (*loca incerta*), forest refuges of souls in torment, unknown

---

*I borrow this word from Old French. It is one of the designations for nightmare, because it corresponds exactly to the German *Aufhocker, Huckupp* in dialect, which designates this kind of figure.

burial places on which a person has walked inadvertently, and so forth. Around the year AD 50, Xenophon of Ephesus tells that a child strayed near the grave of a recently buried man. Someone emerged from the tomb and tried to stop the little girl, who screamed and fled.[21] Jerome Cardan tells us that a Milanese returning home at three in the morning tries to escape a revenant, but the dead one catches him and hurls him to the ground. They struggle, and the man is finally rescued by some passersby, but he dies eight days later.[22] These stories give to us the archetype of the appesart: a wicked dead man who throws himself on you.

The Nightmare

In ancient times the nightmare was an entity covering many different realities: the witch's double that would come and sit heavily on its victim's chest, an oppressively heavy spirit (*mar*) or trampling spirit, or even a dead person.[23] It is closely linked to the appesart but distinct from it in one respect: It attacks sleepers, whereas the appesart hurls itself on travelers and passersby. It strangles men and weighs upon them—like the cobbler who committed suicide in 1591 (see page 69)—and even sucks the blood of the living.[24]

From the end of the sixteenth century to the eighteenth century, the vampire conducted itself like a nightmare, smothering its victims, but this detail has been drowned in the flood of information concerning the vampire's behavior and abusive actions, until we can no longer perceive it. Here again, we see how necessary is a stratigraphic study of the vampire, for it is the only way that allows us to see how we formed the modern myth in which the name *nightmare* keeps recurring. The vampire's sucking causes the same sensation of respiratory distress in its victim. Furthermore, the vampirized individual almost always wonders if he or she has been the prey of a nightmare. When Dr. Seward watches over Lucy Westenra, who is scared to go to sleep, he tells her: "I promise that if I see any evidence of bad dreams I will wake you at once." Moreover, several days earlier, Lucy confides in her personal journal:

I tried to keep awake, and succeeded for a while, but when the clock struck twelve it waked me from a doze, so I must have been falling asleep. There was a sort of scratching or flapping at the window, but I did not mind it, and as I remember no more, I suppose I must have fallen asleep. More bad dreams. I wish I could remember them. This morning I am horribly weak. My face is ghastly pale, and my throat pains me. It must be something wrong with my lungs, for I don't seem to be getting air enough.

Count Dracula had visited her that evening and sucked her blood for the fourth time.

The conflating of the nightmare and the vampire, already pointed out by Ernest Jones, is well illustrated by the Czech *Mora* and the German Alp, two nightmarish entities that suck blood, and if we expand our field of investigation, this notion is confirmed by other creatures, such as the Lapp *ludak,* the Malay *molong,* and the Indo-Chinese *penangelam.*

The Strangler

On January 7, 1732, three Austrian army surgeons handed in to the authorities their report concerning a harmful revenant. Stanoicka, the wife of a *haiduc* [infantry soldier] from Medvegia in Serbia, died at the age of twenty after a three-day illness. Eighteen days after her burial, the doctors J. Fuchinger, J. H. Sigel, and J. F. Baumgarten performed an autopsy and found that her face was rosy red like that of the living and that she had been strangled at midnight by Milloe, the haiduc's son and a vampire. The complete translation of this report can be found in appendix 3. The old texts describing the crimes of vampires indicate that these individuals strangle their victims, which is something that survives in fantasy literature. The victim feels a great sensation of being smothered. The village community discovered that the dead man was a vampire by opening his tomb. He was bathing in an inch of blood, although his role as bloodsucker had yet to evolve to its current extent.

The strangler was therefore already a vampire even if he did not always bear that name.

Charles Ferdinand von Schertz gives a good example of the strangler in his study *Magia posthuma*,[25] from which Dom Calmet borrowed. A deceased woman who had been given all the sacraments—an important detail, because it proves that Christian measures are ineffective—comes back four days after her burial.

> The village inhabitants saw a specter that sometimes appeared in the form of a dog, sometimes that of a man, not one person but several, and caused them much suffering, clutching their throats tightly and compressing their stomachs until they suffocated; it even broke their bodies and reduced them to states of such extreme weakness so that they were visibly pale, thin, and exhausted. The specter even attacked animals, and cows were found struck down and half dead.

Von Schertz does not tell us how they got rid of this plague that lasted several months, but he discusses whether people have the right to incinerate these kinds of revenants.

We should keep in mind the metamorphoses of this female strangler. They are not rare in stories of this nature, and Bram Stoker was undoubtedly inspired by them when he allowed doubt about the true nature of the bat that fluttered before the window of poor Lucy Westenra.

We can note that stranglers often behave like appesarts, as demonstrated in the following anecdote.

> In 1591, a cobbler slit his throat in a famous Silesian town. No one knew why he committed suicide. His wife bandaged the wound and told people he had succumbed to a stroke. At the end of six weeks, a rumor was running through the town: a ghost resembling the cobbler was attacking and crushing sleepers. At the same time another rumor was making the rounds that the cobbler had committed suicide. The dead man's relatives opposed his exhumation, but the dead continued throwing itself on sleepers' beds, grabbing

hold of them and trying to strangle them. He laid upon them so heavily and squeezed them so tightly that pale marks could be seen on their bodies the next morning, and even the impressions of fingers several hours after. Finally the terrified populace had the body, which had been resting in the ground from September 22, 1591, to April 18, 1592, disinterred. It was found that the corpse was intact and quite swollen and that the skin of his feet had fallen off and a new skin grown in. After twenty-four hours, he was buried again but in an ignominious spot. However, the dead man continued his misdeeds until his head, limbs, hands, and feet were cut off on May 7, 1592, and his back was split open. Inside his heart was found to be still intact like that of a freshly slaughtered calf. A pyre was erected with seven cords of wood and the body was cremated. Watch was kept over the ashes that night so that people would not steal them for criminal purposes; the next day, the ashes were placed in a sack and tossed into the river. Henceforth, all was peaceful.[26]

The Chewer

What made the greatest impression upon our ancestors was the sound of chewing jaws coming from the grave,[27] as if the person interred there was devouring something. Dom Calmet gives us one of the definitions of *vampire* during his era, and this definition confirms its kinship if not outright identical nature to this one: "It is said that the vampire experiences a kind of hunger that causes him to eat the grave cloths he finds around him."[28] Latin texts call this type of dead person *manducator,* a neutral term simply descriptive of the phenomenon, whereas the German language uses *Nachzehrer,* which is much more revealing, because it means "one who causes death by devouring something." The corpus regarding this definition is immense and stretches from the fifteenth to the nineteenth centuries, so we have room here for only a few representative examples. We should note from the start that the chewer is a passive vampire, for he does not leave his sepulchre. Rather, he causes death from a distance through sympathetic magic: as he devours or swallows his shroud, those who were close to him in life waste away.

The first testimony is from Inquisitors Jacques Sprenger and Henry Institorus, who were charged with the repression of witchcraft in the Rhineland during the last quarter of the fifteenth century.

> An example was brought to our notice as Inquisitors. A town once was rendered almost destitute by the death of its citizens, and there was a rumor that a certain buried woman was gradually eating the shroud in which she had been buried and that the plague could not cease until she had eaten the whole shroud and absorbed it into her stomach. A council was held and the Podesta with the governor of the city dug up the grave and found half the shroud absorbed through the mouth and throat into the stomach and consumed. In horror at this sight, the Podesta drew his sword and cut off her head and threw it outside the grave and at once the plague ceased.[29]

It is this kind of distinctive dead person that provided later centuries with the fundamental principle of the vampire. The phenomenon was almost always connected to a plague epidemic, without knowing exactly what is meant by this term. Our ancestors attributed all inexplicable deaths to unusual dead people, but this was already the case in Rome where, as Ovid tells us, ancestor worship (*parentalia, dies parentales*) had fallen out of fashion with such noxious consequences that it was quickly restored.[30] The report of the Inquisitors is perhaps not the first of this kind of event. In fact, according to the *Bohemian Chronicle* by Hajek di Libotschan, which goes back to one written by the priest Neplach of Opatowitz around 1370, the case of a chewer was discovered in the Polish village of Lewin Klodzki. Though Neplach makes no mention of "witch," Hajek makes that leap.

> In 1345 the following events took place in the Bohemian town of Lewin. A potter named Duchacz lived there, married to a certain Bradka, who was a witch. When this became known, the priests

urged her to turn away from such spell casting, and although she publicly abstained she continued practicing her craft in secret. One day when she summoned all her spirits, she died brutally and no one could say if she had died a natural death or if the spirits had slain her. For this reason no one wished to bury her among pious Christians and she was interred at a crossroads. It was quite quickly observed that she had come back, often joining the shepherds in the fields by taking the shape of various animals. She terrified the shepherds and chased off their flocks, which caused them many problems. Sometimes she appeared as she did when still alive. Next, she began often coming back to the same town and surrounding villages, entering houses in various guises, speaking to the folk, while terrifying some and slaying a large number. The neighbors in town and the peasants of the surrounding area allied and had her body exhumed by a local skilled in such matters. When this was done, all those present could see that she had eaten half of the veil that had been over her head and it was pulled all covered with blood from her throat. An oak stake was planted in her chest and blood gushed from her body at once, like from a steer, which surprised more than one person, and she was then reburied. A short time later, she began appearing again and much more often than before, terrifying and killing people, then trampling those she slew. For this reason she was once more disinterred by the same man who then found that she had removed the stake that had been planted in her body and was holding it in her hands. Because of this, she was removed from the grave and burned along with her stake, then the ashes were tossed back into the tomb, which was then resealed. For several days a whirlwind was seen where she had been cremated.[31]

This is a complete report and the so-named Bradka is revealed to be both wicked and tough. She is predestined to play this evil role because she is a witch and her death is of the most suspect nature. Not only is she eating her veil, but she also leaves her sepulchre to wander as she pleases. Bradka combined long-vouched-for traits of common revenants:

the ability to metamorphose, the capacity of speech, and a deadly nature. Finally, the testimony clearly tells us that a stake planted in the body is not the correct panacea and that only incineration is effective at putting an end to the wanderings of those like Bradka. Doubt continues to linger, however, because this damned woman succeeded in getting rid of the stake and the whirlwind—a form commonly taken by the soul of the deceased—lasted for a considerable time.

Martin Luther himself was confronted with the problem posed by belief in these wicked dead, and in his *Table Talk* he provides us with the answer to a letter he received.

A pastor named Georg Rörer wrote from Wittenberg that a woman living in a village died and, now that she is buried, she is devouring herself within her tomb, the reason for which all the inhabitants of the village shall soon be dead. He implored Martin Luther for counsel and the latter replied: "This is a diabolical glamour and a malignancy. If they did not believe in it, it would not harm them and they would be convinced that it was no more than an illusion of the devil. But because they are superstitious, they die in greater and greater number. If this was well known, then people would not hurl folk in their graves so impiously but instead say: "Go ahead and eat then, devil! Here's something salty! You don't fool us!'"[32]

The text is sibylline but proves that the phenomenon of the chewers had spread almost everywhere east of the Rhine. Luther's explanation is that of the medieval church—everything is a diabolical illusion— and this theologian believes people can settle the matter by resorting to proven means of exorcism, here represented by the supposedly purifying salt.

According to the *Annals of the City of Wrocław* (Breslau) in Silesia, there was a large-scale mortality in 1517.

From Saint Michael's Day to Saint Andrew's Day around two thousand people died. During this time a shepherd was buried in his clothes in Gross-Mochbar; he devoured them and while doing so made the noise of a sow's jaws. He was therefore disinterred and his blood-covered clothes were found in his mouth; his head was then lopped off with a spade and his body thrown out of the cemetery, at which point the deaths stopped occurring.[33]

This presentation of chewers would be incomplete if we left in the shadows a particularly enlightening text that allows us to establish with certainty the role these out-of-the-ordinary dead played in the crafting of the vampire myth. The Jesuit father Gabriel Rzaczynski confirms the existence of the belief in Poland during the years 1710–1720—which shows that the chewer epidemic was spreading through Europe and that it was this that encouraged the development of what would become a veritable myth. This is what he confides to us:

> I have often heard said by trustworthy witnesses that not only have corpses been found that had long remained uncorrupted, supple, and rosy, but also those whose eyes, tongue, and mouth moved, who had swallowed the shroud in which they had been inhumed and had even devoured parts of their own bodies (*vorare partes sui corporis*). In the meantime, news of a similar corpse had spread, one that has emerged from its tumulus and wandered by crossroads and in front of houses, showing itself sometimes to this person and sometimes to that, and attacking more than one to strangle them. If it involves a man's corpse, the folk call it *upier,* if that of a woman, *upierzyca,* which is almost to say "feathery, light, and moving with agility" (*si veri sit cadaber Upier, si muliebre Upierzyca, quasi dicers plumefactum corpus, leve, agile, ad motum*).[34]

Upier is the original name for vampire, and its use by the recorder therefore establishes a connection between vampires and the chewers and even the stranglers. We will revisit this name a little later, because the interpretation offered here, which makes the vampire an entity resembling the stirges of classical antiquity, is at first glance stupefying. Rzaczynski adds that these corpses are decapitated to prevent them from attacking people. Starting in 1730, the authorities began to become concerned about these repeated exhumations and the profanations of sepulchres, which were accompanied by "barbarous actions." Thus, in that year, the Alsfeld authorities in Hesse prohibited the disinterment and impalement of a dead person heard chewing in his or her grave. In Austria-Hungary, as we saw earlier, a writ dated 1755 and issued by Maria Teresa provided the legal basis for the banning of posthumous executions.

Revenants in Animal Form

We have met on several occasions the dead that can transform themselves—although, alas, not into bats, as Bram Stoker claims. In his novel he introduces this flying creature as well as wolves and dogs. In fact, however, quite a number of other beasts were the subject of the dead's metamorphosis. In the *Chronicle of Frankenstein,* Martin Kolbitz notes for the year 1605:

> In spring and summer here in Neustadt and elsewhere in many places, a monster has shown itself, often in the shape of a dog, sometimes that of a calf, during the night before and after midnight. This animal is called the Rothe or the Drothe. It has persecuted people terribly on the road that leads from Baumgarten to Frankenberg, near the woods. It has shown itself to travelers in full daylight and leaped upon them, like a large skittle; it has violently tormented passersby to such an extent none dare take this road; when the miller, Martin Riedeln, took it, he was molested so savagely that he died from it three days later.[35]

We should not allow ourselves to be led astray by the word *monster.* It means revenant and is the equivalent of the Latin *monstrum,* which holds the same meaning. In folk beliefs east of the Rhine, this revenant that throws itself on passersby was also called *Aufhocker* (appesart). Its weight was practically intolerable, and the person who had been attacked remained for some time in such a weakened state that death can be the result. The wicked dead thing of Neustadt takes various forms, but this is nothing new because, since around 1200, we have encountered metamorphosing revenants—and testimonies about them multiplied in the fifteenth century. The most common animal forms were the dog, the goat, the crow, and the horse, and other forms could be a ball of fire or even a burning bush. Each region of Europe has developed its own representations. In an era closer to our own, it was claimed that these revenants also appeared as fleas, lice, and ticks—parasites that are of course vampiric.

We have now familiarized ourselves with vampires but have not yet examined their names. Because it is common knowledge that there is always a close connection between any concept and its appellation, it will not be a waste of time to scrutinize vampires' names in the next chapter.

5

Names of the Vampire

In the records are such words as "stregoica" witch,
"ordog" and "pokol" Satan and hell, and in one
manuscript this very Dracula is spoken of as
"wampyr" . . .

BRAM STOKER, *DRACULA*

UP TO THIS POINT, various hypotheses have been formulated on the meaning and etymology of the word *vampire*. Linguistic origin is important because we know that a word generally offers an explanation for the deepest levels of the semantic strata and provides keys that allow for the opening of sometimes unexpected perspectives. There is a proverb that says *Nomen est numen*.* As early as 1909, Joseph Klapper demonstrated that the name encompassed a plurality of different individuals, but his efforts at clarification appear to have remained dead, and people have continued using the term without much care about exactitude, especially because most books on this subject target more the fans of the sensational and the irrational than those minds that have a genuine desire to learn.

---

*[To name is to know. —*Trans.*]

Concerning Witches and Werewolves

In Istria the vampire was called *strigon,* a word in which we can recognize *strige* or *stirge,* which in ancient times meant "witch" or *vedarez.* In the Balkans we have *vampir; wampir* in Poland; and in the Carpathians *opyr,* which in Russian means "suspended death" (*zaloznyj pokojnik*). The Kachubs used *upor* and the Czechs *upir.* The Polish and Kachub used *wieszczy,* "the announcer." *Vischun* was used in Dalmatia, underscoring a certain science and therefore falling under the heading of magic and sorcery, which is confirmed by another word: *strzysz,* "wizard." The Bulgarian *dedejo* established a link between the vampire and the world of the ancestors, while *platnik,* "flesh," evoked its physical nature. In Croatia the appellations of the vampire were *vukodlak, ukodlak,* and *vuk*—and these seem based on "wolf" and mean "wolf's fur," which brings us back to the notion of werewolf (but opinions diverge on this point). We know, though, that there is an amazing kinship between the vampire and the werewolf, and in Ukraine and Byelorussia [Belarus] it was thought that vampires were men who were werewolves during their lifetime.

Vârkolac

In the nineteenth century, the Russian-Latin dictionaries defined *vârkolac* as "lunar eclipse" (*ecclypsis lunae*) and as "specter formed by a corpse and a demon." These two terms of the definition refer to the werewolf and to the animation of a cadaver by a malefic entity. For seven years, the vârkolac rested in its burial place, then it left in the form of a small black child who sucked the blood of human beings. It would return to its victim's home in several weeks or several months, and the victim would feel exhausted and start slowly wasting away. A small red patch was visible on the victim's left arm, an obvious clue to the attacker's nature. If the vârkolac mades nine visits to a person and sucked his blood, its target would die in a matter of a few days, a detail Bram Stoker used in *Dracula:* Lucy Westenra's blood is sucked nine times, and she survives only for a time thanks to transfusions. The vârkolac was particularly dangerous because it was able to reduce its size at will in order to enter rooms through the keyholes. It was also said to be the seventh or ninth child of the same couple, and it possessed the ability to change into an animal when it wished. In this animal form, it then returned to sleepers to suck their blood.[1]

The close connection that exists among the werewolves of the southern Slavs is confirmed by the beliefs found in this geographical area. Werewolves found no rest after their deaths and devoured the flesh of their own hands and feet—then, when they had nothing left to eat, they left their graves at midnight, attacking flocks, breaking in to houses, and lying on top of sleepers and sucking their blood. Once they were restored, they returned to their burial places. Their victims bore a bite mark either at the breast or at the level of the heart.[2]

Grobnik

In Bulgaria we encounter the term *grobnik,* formed from *grob,* "the grave," and *tenee,* derived from *ten,* "shadow." We also have *lepir,* which designated a dead person of unknown origin and was often confused with *ustrel,* a demon that inhabited graves, and with *morava,* a demon of illnesses that tormented men at night. For its part, the Polish *morus,* from the Latin *mors,* simply indicateed that a person was dead.

Opyr

Opyr, which we have seen used by Sheridan Le Fanu in his book in the form *upyre,* does not have a certain etymology. It has been compared to the Serbian verb *piriti,* "to swell," and the Greek *apyros,* "not harmed by fire," as well as to the Turkish *pir* (*per*), "to fly," which can be found again in northern Tunisia in the form of *uber,* "vampire." In favor of this Oriental hypothesis, scholars have dwelled on the Polish verb *upierzyc,* "to endow with feathers," and *upior,* "winged phantom," which is reminiscent of the strigi and other empusae of classical antiquity.

The semantic field of *vampire* gravitates around the notions we find continuously in the testimonies: the three-dimensional dead person, the dead who has not "passed away," the wizard, and the man who possesses the ability to change into a wolf.

Vourdalak

Alexei Tolstoy uses the term *vourdalak.*

> The *vourdalaks* (the name given to vampires by Slavic peoples) are, according to local folklore, dead bodies who rise from their graves to suck the blood of the living. In this respect, they behave like all types of vampires, but they have one other characteristic that makes them even more terrifying. The *vourdalaks* prefer to suck the blood of their closest relatives and their most intimate friends; once dead the victims become vampires themselves. People have claimed that entire villages in Bosnia and Hungary have been transformed into *vourdalaks* this way.

We should be aware straight off that *vourdalak* was not a term from Russian beliefs. It entered the vocabulary thanks to Pushkin, who employed it exclusively in the poems "Marco Jakubovitz" and "Vurdalak," which form part of *Song of the Western Slavs,* a cycle that is itself the translation of a book by Prosper Merimée, *Guzla ou Poèmes illyriens.* It is, in fact, a Croatian and Dalmatian word, and Pushkin takes the trouble to add a footnote to his poems to explain the word: "The *vurdalak, vudkodlak, upyr* are dead who leave their graves and suck the blood of the living."[3] In this way, we can observe the role literature can play in the propagation of this belief.

Broucolaca

For his part, Dom Augustin Calmet uses the word *broucolaka* or *brucolaca.* The two words come from Greece, where they have formed the word *vrikolakas,* which designated a zombie or revenant that attacks livestock.[4] In 1721 the bishop of Avranches gave us his etymology of the term: "The word *brucolaca* comes from the modern Greek *bourcos,* which means 'mud,' and *laucos,* which means 'ditch,' 'sewer,' because, as we are assured, the graves in which these bodies have been placed are ordinarily found filled with mud."[5] The Byelorussians [Belarusians] in fact used the term *mjertovjec,* "the walking dead," to designate vampires. These individuals may have been werewolves or wizards or even excommunicates cursed by the clergy or by their kin. They walked or rode, made noises with their bones, terrified the living, and vanished at the third cock crow. When their tombs were opened, they could be recognized at once because they were lying flat on their belly. If a person encountered them, they could be identified immediately by their nose, which is missing its bone, and their split lower lip.

Nosferat

Bram Stoker used *nosferatu,* a name made famous by the film by F. W. Murnau (1922) in which Max Schreck incarnated Count Dracula, but he in fact blended different figures from Romanian folk beliefs: the *nosferat* properly speaking (a revenant), the *murony* of Wallachia, the *strigoï,* the *moroiu,* and the *stafiu,* about which I must say a few words, because they are not among the creatures known to the public at large.

Murony

Like the nosferat, the murony of Wallachia was the illegitimate offspring of two illegitimate children or the harmful spirit of a person slain by a vampire. By day, it slept in the grave; at night, it moved freely wherever desire took it and sucked the blood of the living. It was immortal and could be destroyed only if its body, which could be recognized by its ruddy complexion in the coffin, was burned or was disinterred, a needle was stuck in its forehead, and a stake was driven through its heart. It was believed that the murony could transform into a dog, cat, toad, frog, louse, flea, bedbug, or spider. It would not necessarily leave a mark on the throat of the person whose blood it had been sucking, which reinforces the fear people felt in the presence of a sudden death.

The nosferat, however, was often a stillborn child. Once it had been buried, it came to life and left its grave, never to return. It could change into a dog or a cat—most often black—a beetle, a butterfly, and even a wisp of straw. It would suck the blood of the elderly and copulate with women. Its victims grew thin, wasted away, and died. When a child was born from these unnatural couplings, it was hideous and covered with hair. After its death, it created a *moroiu,* about which we shall speak later in this chapter.

Strigoï

The Romanian *strigoï* had two meanings: "witch," when it involved living women, and "revenant," when it designated men who seemed dead or cadavers that did not rot, either because they possessed two souls—a good one that left the body at the moment of death and an evil one that remained—or because the soul had returned to inhabit its carnal envelope six weeks, six months, or seven years after death.[6] These revenants had the same appearance they held in life, though they were sometimes bigger in size, had red eyes, fingernails like sickles, a hairy tail, and a large mouth. Their face was ruddy because they sucked much blood, their legs and their hands were thin and dry like spindles, or they had the feet of horses or geese. They walked about barefoot, clad in a red or white shirt or completely naked. Their bodies were hairy, their hair was long, and they had very large teeth. They were sometimes depicted as skeletons covered with skin, sometimes as burly dwarves. They left their tombs at midnight, carrying their caskets on their heads or backs, and wherever they went, they brought cholera, pestilence, and diseases affecting livestock. They ate the hearts of man and beast, sucked their blood, and drained the souls from their kinfolk. If they landed on someone when metamorphosed into a fly, that person would die. They liked to frequent houses, cemeteries, land under bridges, crossroads, and remote places. They danced on graves and flew around bell towers, singing and shouting, and witches took part in these activities with them. They fought among each other with stalks of flax, axes, sickles, and so forth, and the winner was named king of the revenants. If someone passed within the proximity of this battle, the revenants would strike him and make him forget what he was intending to do. Whoever passed by the next day would see much spilled blood and lose the power to speak. After being defeated in such battles, the revenants gathered in an abandoned house, spun stolen wool, and wove linen shirts. Their principle assembly took place on the night of St. Andrew [November 30]. The strigoï went back into their graves at dawn or when vespers were rung. If they delayed, they would burst into two pieces or could be killed.

Moroiu

Let's take a look at the *moroiu* that Paul Wilson resuscitates and brings into the present day in his book *The Keep.* Originally, the moroiu was a heavy, cumbersome spirit, an appesart. It was born from a child who had died before being baptized or who was stillborn. Many of these individuals were illegitimate children whom their mothers had killed and buried outside of the cemetery. Seven years after birth, the soul of such a child would shout from the grave: "Baptism, baptism!" If someone heard it and spoke the baptismal ritual formula, gave it a name, and tossed a piece of cloth as a gift toward the spot from where the shout was heard, the child was baptized and would no longer be a moroiu. If his cry was not heard or if the rite was not performed, the child would transform into a six-foot flame soaring over the surface of the ground. If it touched a living being, it would kill it, and if it collided with a building, it would set it on fire. It was also said that it could take the form of a cat that attacked travelers, a hare that bit them, or a red flame that rendered them mute, mad, or simply ill.

The graves of these children were sprinkled with holy water on Epiphany for seven years in a row. In this way the little ones were symbolically baptized and could therefore find eternal rest. Take note! A moroiu is worse than a demon because it cannot be banished by the sign of the cross. It can appear at midnight as a woman wearing a white linen cloth over her chest, therefore as a kind of white lady, and it will disfigure any person it encounters. The southwestern Romanians made no distinction between the moroiu and the revenant. According to several traditions from this region, those dead that became moroiu were disinterred, and in order to get rid of them, their hearts were plucked from their bodies and cast to the dogs.

Stafia

The *stafia* was a malefic being that came to life in this fashion: When masons secretly measured the shadow of a man or animal that fell upon a building and buried the measure in the foundations of the building to prevent its possible collapse, these living creatures died when the building was completed or shortly after losing their shadow. They then became stafi. Contrary to revenants, they had no body and no tail and were bound to this site, appearing only where their shadow had been buried. Murder victims and suicides could also become stafi.

In folk traditions the stafia resembled a woman whose hair touched the ground and whose chest was immensely long and made from iron. The woman appeared naked or clad in white, was very thin and very ugly, and was as pale as a wax taper. Her eyes looked like onions, her mouth a plate, her head looked like a bucket, her ears like sponges, and her teeth like a wool carder. The stafia also came in the guise of an animal (pig, dog, cat, ram, billy goat, nanny goat, horse, and so on). It loomed up at night in homes, cellars, and churches, on bridges, in abandoned springs, in deserted places, at crossroads, and in the forest. Generally speaking, it was not wicked, but the wicked ones would beat an individual with their chest and would scratch, strangle, and drive the breath from sleepers or mutilate them. They blew out candles and looked for food in houses. To propitiate them, people left them food and drink in easily accessible locations.

Vampir

Vampir was mentioned for the first time east of the Rhine in 1732, and the author who used the term, about whom we only know the initials of his name, was wondering about the meaning of the word.[7] In England *vampyre* entered the vocabulary through the channel of a travel narrative published in 1745 but written in 1734: *The Travels of Three English Gentlemen, from Venice to Hamburg.*[8] The narrator cites cases of vampirism in Serbia, the Banat region, Russia, Poland, and Lithuania, based on the text of the headmaster Johann Heinrich Zopf,[9] and writes: "The vampires" are supposed to be the cadavers of deceased people animated by evil spirits, "which come out of their graves in the night-time, rush upon people sleeping in their beds, suck out all their blood and destroy them."

If it were necessary to draw up a balance sheet of the names of the dead cited in this chapter, we could say that all these individuals had many points in common as well as many differences. The borders between them remained indistinct: there is more than one overlap that can be explained initially by the geographical origins of each and by the confusion that rules in human minds. Over the course of time, precise data lost their hard edges, and the tendency we have already noted with respect to the precursors of the vampire was upheld: the blends and combinations tended to diminish the dissimilarities and glossed over the differences. Nonetheless, one fact remains: these human bloodsuckers were reputedly real and must be eliminated in order to lead a peaceful life.

6

How Do We Protect Ourselves from Vampires?

Loves, Loves,
The heart comes in and shouting,
To make itself heard at judgment,
It protests against you:
Rabbits, snakes, and deer.
Isn't hunting a good thing?
Human hearts
Wherever they are found is where they are lost.
It is their blood that soothes me,
It is their flesh that nourishes me,
And that is how I live!

ADRIEN CREMENE,
"NIGHT SONG OF THE VAMPIRE"

THE PROTECTION AGAINST vampires could be performed at three different times: when they have just been born, during their death, or sometime after they have given up their souls and have become the guests of an intermediary world that is no longer that of life or of death. Other measures aimed to protect the home against this permanent menace.

Suspect Births

Certain signs of birth, which were mentioned in chapter 3, could reveal the advent of a vampire: a monstrous birth, for example, was a harmful sign (*portentum*) that inspired the utilization of draconian measures, especially when the nature of the father could be questioned. He could be a vampire; a revenant who had sexual relations with his wife; or an undefined spirit, a devil from the succubus family[1]—which was the primary explanation offered by clerics from the Middle Ages to the sixteenth century. Because a good example is worth more than a long explanation, one of our ancestors reported the following:

In 1565, a woman from Schmitz, a village under the jurisdiction of the noble lord Vratislaus of Bernstein, gave birth to a diabolical being that had no head or feet. On its chest, near the left shoulder it bore a mouth, and near its right shoulder, an ear. It had suction cups instead of fingers, like a frog or toad; its entire body was the color of liver and shook like lard or jelly. When the midwife set this being into a tub seat or basin to wash it, it emitted the most horrible cries. Many people came and looked at this creature in front of the church; then it was buried in a spot reserved for children who died without receiving baptism, but his mother did not cease asking that this terrible being be dug up and totally destroyed so that nothing remained. She confessed that she had had frequent relations with a devil who had taken the appearance of her husband. It was necessary to restore to this devil what was his and to immediately procure for her, who Satan had so terrified and tormented, women to watch over her, and pious and loyal friends. On the orders of His Lordship, Vratislaus, the aborted child was exhumed, placed on a cart, and given to the executioner to burn outside the village. Despite the enormous quantity of wood burned, it proved impossible to annihilate this diabolical mass; even the cloths in which it had been swaddled remained damp despite the heat of the raging flames, until the executioner cut it into tiny pieces and destroyed them in the fire with the greatest difficulty. This took place on the Friday after Ascension. During this time, the devil tormented the woman violently. That night, a noise like horses could be heard making a great clatter around her house, accompanied by the noise of bells, and then plaintive moans on the following night, first beneath her windows and then in the house itself, which terrified the mother and her neighbors. The woman continually prayed to God and the Church to intercede for her; that someone put an end to her torment by commanding the devil to sink back into the deepest level of Hell. A great howling was then heard, as if dogs and cats were fighting each other tooth and nail, a loud ringing of bells, and the river that flowed alongside her house then overflowed, to the great displeasure of her neighbors. But the pious prayers finally delivered the woman from the wrath and spite of the insane devil, through the grace of divine mercy.[2]

Beneath this Christian interpretation of the facts, it is easy to recognize the "reality": a dead man came back to visit his wife and made a child with her. The rest of the story smacks of exemplary literature or a sermon. Thanks to the measures taken, they managed to cut short a future scourge: the aborted child did not have time to transform into a vampire, and the community was saved.

Precautions during Death and Burial

In addition to the well-known general precautionary measures taken to provide protection against the dead—such as biting the big toe of the corpse so it would not come back, keeping vigil over it to protect it from any evil spirits lying in wait or from witches who desired to

procure from it ingredients for their spells,[3] making it understand*
that it had passed away,[4] removing the body through a hole in the
wall cut specially for this purpose, trying to lead it astray by making
a thousand turns and detours between his house and the cemetery,
or by taking the body over running water or crossroads—precautions
that applied to all those whose return is dreaded, there are others that
more specifically concerned putative vampires. In 1719 a medical peri-
odical devoted a brief note to the various beliefs surrounding burials.
In this, we can read the precautions people took at this time.

> May we be permitted to cite in passing one or more of the super-
> stitions concerning cadavers and inhumations. These, for example,
> signify what is called the return of the dead, the oozing of blood
> from a dead body, the incorruptible nature of the bodies of this or
> that kind of sinner, the so-called vampirism, the howling of dogs
> the dropping of the *bayart* [the funeral stretcher], the absence of any
> cadaverous rigidity in the body of the one who just died, and other
> common physical interpretations, the opening of a window at the
> time of death, the fear of wetting the shroud with tears, paying the
> carpenter for the coffin without breaking a penny, if one or more
> of the mortuary candles goes out, and many other similar events.
> Wouldn't these be superstitions?[5]

The signs mentioned in the extract were widespread throughout
Europe, but they were interpreted as heralds of the transformation of
the dead individual into a vampire. They were linked to the category of
nonicides and chewers, those passive vampires that caused death from a
distance, without leaving their graves. In 1800 the pastor of Steinkirch
recorded his observations on the death of his daughter and notes "that
particular attention must be paid to ensure that no ribbon or clothing is
left near the mouth of the departed, otherwise she will chew on it in the

---

*One watcher at a wake boasted she had pushed down by force one dead individual who
rose up from his bed, and she told the dead one: "Eh! What do you think you are doing
among the living? Lie down! You are no longer one of us."

grave until a member of the family passes away." This precaution can be found throughout Germany.[6]

What was most dreaded is what we could call the contagion of death—something that took a wide variety of forms of which vampires are but one facet. We can count fifteen hundred beliefs from east of the Rhine during the eighteenth and nineteenth centuries that give us a small glimpse of the precautions taken against such signs:[7]

- When a corpse has a red face, one of the friend's of the deceased will die shortly.
- Tears that fall on a dead body prevent it from resting in peace.
- Scissors and a sewing box with needles, thread, and spool should be given to a woman who died in labor to prevent her from coming back to look for them (Pforzheim, 1787).
- The deceased lying on a funeral stretcher should not have an end of the shroud in his mouth (Wurtemberg, 1788).
- The peaceful rest of the dead individual requires that every person present around the grave should throw three clumps of dirt in it (Ansbach, 1786).
- A clump of dirt or a small wooden board should be placed beneath the mouth of the dead person to prevent him from grabbing the shroud with his teeth and luring his kin to his side (Ansbach, 1786).
- If a corpse sighs on the hay on which it has been laid; if the corpse remains limber; if it swallows a ribbon, a shroud, or a closed end, a family member will soon follow it into the grave.
- Shouting the name of the dead person will wake him.
- The gravedigger must dig the hole on the day of the burial in order for the dead individual to leave in peace.
- If, by chance, the funeral veils are placed backward on the hearse, a member of the household of the deceased will soon perish.

Essential data stand out in the background of these beliefs: the notion of sacrifice or gift (the clumps of dirt), of life in the beyond (the sewing kit), of order (the correct placement of the funeral decorations), and of the danger of the dead person transforming into a chewer. We should add that if the ends of the corpse's fingers turned blue, a close relative would soon perish; anyone talking about the dead person should always have added "God keep him!" or a phrase that has the same meaning; if the name of the deceased was called three times, he would appear; and the cadaver remained dangerous for a period of forty days—or up to a year, according to the Russians—because during this time, the deceased could return to visit his home.

At the beginning of the twentieth century, a survey was carried out throughout Germany. It was conducted by the publishers of the *Atlas der deutschen Volkskunde* (Atlas of German Ethnology), who sent questionnaires everywhere and made a summary of the answers.[8] This survey enables us to observe the perennial nature of these beliefs. To the question "How can you recognize a dead person who is going to transform into a wicked being that lures the living to him?" there were fifty-six responses. Although the survey did not specifically address vampires, fifty responses pertain to this subject, while the remaining six concern the position of the gravedigger's spade (which indicates who will be the next to die). Here are the pertinent responses and their number:

- The body's eyes remain open: 14
- The body's mouth remains open: 1
- The body remains limber, keeps its color, smiles: 17
- The grave dirt does not settle: 15
- Someone stumbles over an open grave: 3

Another way of protecting yourself from these monsters was to use Christian charms, and the one cited most often is the Ticket of St. Luke, as in this testimony from 1801:

The body of Marguna Warlin, inhabitant of Ulischko, was carried to Gross-Gorschütz, in the Oderberg District, to be buried there. Rumor was running that this woman had a chisel in her back and was therefore a so-called vampire, so the local pastor placed a death notice [the Ticket of St. Luke] beneath her tongue, stuffed her nostrils with earth, and had her laid on her stomach in the coffin, with her face turned toward the ground, and buried her without any ceremony.[9]

Different measures are implemented here, which proves people harbored doubt about the charm's efficacy, generally used to cure illnesses. Patients were made to eat a note—a ticket—on which was inscribed:

J†N†R†J

et verbum ca

co factum est

et habitavit

in nobis.[10]

Christian measures were the most numerous.[11] There was the aspersion with holy water whose purpose William Durand, bishop of Mende in the thirteenth century, defined this way: the aim was not to "repel the sins of the departed but to repress the presence of all the vile spirits." Wax from a blessed candle was dripped on the navel of the corpse, and three small wax crosses or salt were placed on the body or a metallic object (such as an iron, open scissors, keys, pliers, a sickle) was placed near it. Sometimes a heavy ax or a stone or pewter spoons were placed on the coffin lid. Other precautions were obviously intended to hamper the freedom of the de cujus: His hands might be tied behind his back or the body might be tied to the stretcher. In Denmark, the two big toes were tied together with red thread, or the legs were tied together with black silk thread after needles had been stuck in the soles of the feet.

Because the movement of the corpse's jaws would cause more deaths, attempts were made to prevent this by tying the mouth of the deceased—a measure inspired by reality, for this procedure was followed while waiting for rigor mortis to end—or by placing inside the mouth a coin or a tile fragment or a stone that the dead person would chew with no harmful consequences to the living. It does seem, in fact, that mortality was essentially connected to the devouring of the shroud or that of the corpse's own limbs. The jaws were also kept from moving up and down by placing beneath the chin of the deceased a clump of dirt or a piece of aspen on which three crosses had been carved. Michael Ranft, to whom I owe this information, adds that the throat of the corpse was also bound quite tightly with a handkerchief to prevent it from swallowing.

> In fact, there are people who place a clump of freshly dug earth beneath the chin of the corpses during burial to prevent the dead from chewing, with all its disastrous effects. In Dresden, it is customary to bind the corpse securely with a handkerchief or scarf, solely to prevent the physical possibility of mastication. Müller . . . mentions the undertakers' habit of placing a clump of dirt beneath the chins of the deceased, and he does not disapprove of it.[12]

Finally, the dead had to be removed from his house feet first so that he could not cast a final look at his home and thereby have the desire to return.

The most ancient method of prevention for which there is evidence— it is encountered even as early as the Neolithic era—is the burial of the body flat on its stomach, its mouth turned toward the ground.[13] This particular form of inhumation is well known to archaeologists, and evidence for it can be found throughout Europe. It has been discovered in Germany and Hungary as well as in Normandy, Lorraine, and the Languedoc. Placing the body with its mouth facing the ground was the means for diverting malefic energy: instead of escaping from the tomb, it would bury itself in the earth. Furthermore, if the dead person was a chewer, the first thing he would devour would be the dirt, and people would be safe. On certain occasions it served as a kind of posthumous expiation, as in the case of Pepin the Short who, according to the *Chronicle of Saint Denis,* was buried this way in order to redeem the sins of his own father, Charles Martel.[14] It was applied to all malefactors and criminals—it was a form of exile from the community—and to suicides who had transgressed against God by killing themselves. We should recall that usually the dead are buried on the back—called *dorsal decubitus* in the Middle Ages—with the head pointed toward the west. Suicides, considered self-murderers, received a *sepultura asini,* a dishonorable burial. This postmortem punishment was also intended to prevent the dead from becoming a member of the community of the dead: the criminal or evil man was treated beyond the grave just as he was treated in the land of the living—he met the same ostracism. We should note, however, that burial flat on the belly cannot necessarily always be interpreted this way, because it was also used by the Dominicans of Guebwiller.[15] It could be a mark of humility and could depict the dead person in prayer. It is in fact known that some monks followed the custom of praying in church while lying flat on their bellies.

If the deceased was a hanged man, a potentially wicked dead man, the rope and the beam it was strung on were placed in his grave. If this was not done, the dead man would return every evening, rapping on windows and shouting, "Give me the wood!" No one would get any peace until this was done. In order to prevent dead people from becoming revenants (strigoï), cloves of garlic were placed in their coffin and in their mouth, nose, and ears. When the deceased was a marginal individual, he had to be carried far from the village and buried successively at three crossroads. If this did not work, the corpse was burned or even banished, as was the case with an inhabitant of Riegersdorf around 1900. In Romania, if the dead individual was suspected of being a werewolf (*varkolac*), a thorn-covered branch was placed in his shroud. The idea was that it would hold him back if he entertained any notions of wandering outside his grave. The moroiu's grave, meanwhile, had to be doused with a decoction of helianthemum (rock rose). The dead person could also be provided with a task: poppy seeds could be placed in his coffin, and he would have to count them before he could leave, or a stocking or net could be buried with him, and he had to unstitch it entirely before he could leave. Considering, however, that he could undo the stitching only at a rate of one stitch per year, the living were guaranteed years of tranquillity.

To prevent the transformation of the dead into a revenant, and more specifically into a vampire, the corpse was treated in a variety of ways. Incense was placed in the nostrils to prevent the dead person from breathing, in the ears so he could not hear Satan, in the eyes to prevent him from seeing, and in the mouth so he could not reveal the name of his kin to the demon—all measures founded on the belief that a devil possessed the body and animated it. Sometimes, garlic was placed in the mouth and anus or pebbles, peas, and grains of wheat were placed in the orifices of the body. Sometimes nine stones were arranged in the coffin, or dog roses, braided rushes, a polenta spoon, and a hawthorn cross were placed on the chest. If the dead person was suspected of turning into a revenant, sprigs of basil, wine, incense, an egg, iron nails, sand, or hawthorn might have been placed in the casket. The heart might have been impaled with oak, ash, or yew. The surviving brother of the same month had to enter and leave the tomb of his dead brother three times so that the deceased did not devour him.

Sometimes, the head of the dead person was cut off and placed at its feet in the grave—a measure practiced throughout medieval Europe. In Wallachia a heavy stone was placed on top of the deceased's head. In the suburbs of Danzig (Gdansk), a woman was buried at a crossroads around 1820. She had been decapitated and her head placed beneath her arm. Farther to the west, near Gandersheim, the tongue of the dead person would be nailed to the mouth. Elsewhere, veritable crucifixions were common: The hands and feet were nailed to the coffin and the body was impaled on a stake or a long needle. Sometimes, the dead individual was nailed inside his casket, the nails driven through it entirely.

When the dead person was a wizard, the measures were multiplied. William of Malmesbury (ca. 1080–1142) recorded for us the final wishes of a Berkeley witch. Fearing that devils would carry off her corpse, she asks of her children:

> You may be able to preserve my body in the following fashion: wrap me in the hide of a stag, then place me in a stone sarcophagus and seal its lid with lead and iron; surround this stone mass with three iron chains that are as heavy as possible, and order that fifty psalmists recite psalms for me at night and as many say Mass for me at day, to

fend off the violent irruptions of my adversaries. If my body remains undisturbed for three nights, then you may place your mother in the earth, although I fear it may be loath to keep me in its depths, she who has made it so often bear the weight of my misdeeds.[16]

These precautions proved futile, and demons carried off the corpse. Behind the Christinization of this event, we can read the belief that a dead person such as this one could return and could therefore present a danger to the living, hence the attempt to seal the coffin so hermetically that the witch would be unable to get out. Because the stag is the symbol for Christ in Christian symbology, the creature's skin served as an obstacle to all evil spells; it was a true phylactery and even an exorcism. As for the iron, there is another dimension to it besides its use as chains: it was reputed to send spirits fleeing.

We should note that impalement was not reserved only for vampires. Once upon a time, it was initially applied to sorcerers—quite often, combined with other measures, such as decapitation. At the beginning of the thirteenth century, Saxo Grammaticus gives us something that is very similar to the reports from subsequent centuries. After a certain Mithothyn had been buried:

> . . . his infamy became most evident inasmuch, it is passing strange, as all those who went near his tomb died suddenly. Furthermore, pestilential miasmas emanated from their corpses. . . . Beset by this scourge, the inhabitants tore the dead man from his tomb, cut off his head and pierced his chest with a pointed stake. It was in this way that the people put an end to their misfortunes.[17]

After the Burial

In eastern and central Europe, three days after the interment people placed on the grave three, five, or nine spindles or oakum, which was then set alight. Those performing this rite sowed peas or poppies on the return path while saying, "The dead man will come back only when these seeds return to the house," or even, "May the revenant eat one of these seeds every year and not the hearts of his kinfolk!" I will mention only Christian rites such as the *trentain,* a funeral service celebrated on the thirtieth day after the death. Its purpose is to facilitate the passage of the departed into the beyond. Other commemorative ceremonies were intended to give satisfaction to the dead individual.

In Bulgaria the vampire was considered harmful to his parentage as well as to his native group. It was therefore necessary to liquidate him. He remained identifiable and locatable by his kin and neighbors during the annual cycle following the death date, when the commemoration rituals were celebrated three, nine, or forty days after his decease, or even in the six months and year that followed. As time passed he became less and less identifiable, and once the year had passed, he could emigrate, build himself a new life, marry, and have children—motifs that appear in Polidori's novella in which Lord Ruthven is bound in holy matrimony to Aubrey's sister.

Protection of the Home

When Dr. Abraham van Helsing seeks to protect Lucy Westenra from the bites of Count Dracula, he brings in a large clump of flowering garlic and proceeds in this fashion:

> The Professor's actions were certainly odd and not to be found in any pharmocopeia that I ever heard of. First he fastened up the windows and latched them securely. Next, taking a handful of the flowers, he rubbed them all over the sashes, as though to ensure that every whiff of air that might get in would be laden with the garlic smell. Then with the wisp he rubbed all over the jamb of the door, below, and at each side, and round the fireplace in the same way.

The purpose of this was to prohibit the vampire's entry by sealing with garlic any opening through which he might slip. This procedure was only one of the measures formerly used against revenants in general.

To keep the vârkolac at bay, the Romanians recommended arranging garlic, fennel, and incenses in the bed, drawing crosses above it with the ash procured from the incense burner, or drawing Seals of Solomon—that is, pentagrams that were known east of the Rhine as "witch's feet" and had a reputation for dispelling nightmares. Yet these measures worked as well against other revenants and against witches, which could be held at bay by, on certain dates, rubbing with garlic all the doors, windows, chimneys, cracks, and so on in a house. All the plates would be turned over and the household would eat garlic, because the returning dead were unable to tolerate its smell. Against the moroiu, the Romanians, for example, would rub the gates, doors, window frames, and all smoke outlets (or chimneys) with three heads of garlic borrowed from three different houses while repeating the following ritual spell: "Moroiu, leave my domain and never dare again return to soil my place, my animals, and my dwelling, my children, and myself! Go to the deserted regions, go back into your grave from whence you came, and never come out again. Amen."

In Denmark the old wheel of a spinning wheel would be hung over the door to a farmhouse because it was believed that the dead man could enter only after having walked around the building for as many times as that wheel had turned. Almost everywhere in western Europe, the door of the house would be slammed after the wake or two axes were stuck in the ground to form a cross on the boundary line of the property.

You now have the *vade mecum* of the vampire hunter. Yet individuals who are ignorant of the information they can use to protect themselves and do not know how to take the appropriate measures are confronted with difficulty: a sudden unexpected death, which necessitates seeking out its causes and origin.

7

Identifying and Killing the Vampire

Joy in the presence of death belongs only to he for which there is no beyond.

GEORGES BATAILLE

FORTUNATELY, THERE ARE several means for identifying vampires, and Dr. Abraham van Helsing is not the lone expert in the matter. Broadly speaking, we must distinguish four stages corresponding to the phases of manifestation: deaths in quick succession, the identification of the vampire, the opening of the crypt, and the execution.

Deaths in Quick Succession

The first stage is initiated by a sign that cannot be misconstrued: A person in the neighborhood wastes away or else several deaths occur in rapid succession for no visible reason. The cause is thought to be an epidemic or a pestilence, as it was once called. As the hermit says in Alexei Tolstoy's *The Family of the Vourdalak:* "Vampirism is contagious; many people have been stricken by it, and many families have died out to their last member." Le Fanu explains how this calamity is able to spread.

Assume, at starting, a territory perfectly free from that pest. How does it begin, and how does it multiply itself? I will tell you. A person, more or less wicked, puts an end to himself. A suicide, under certain circumstances, becomes a vampire. That specter visits living people in their slumbers; *they* die, and almost invariably, in the grave, develop into vampires.

In the eighteenth century, Monsieur de l'Isle de Saint-Michel noted:

A person finds himself assailed by languor, loses his appetite, visibly loses weight, and, at the end of eight to ten days, sometimes fifteen, dies without fever and no other symptom of illness other than gauntness and emaciation. In Hungary it is said that these are signs that a vampire has attached itself to this person and is sucking his blood. Of those who are attacked by this dark melancholy, the majority, troubled in mind, believe they see a white specter following them everywhere, like the shadow follows the body.[1]

Therefore, there is not a shadow of a doubt that men of earlier times interpreted events that would be blindingly clear to us through the lens of a long tradition of beliefs. This is how the belief in vampires spread, but in all likelihood, with the cause of death was a simple epidemic, which these folks called a plague for lack of any precise diagnosis.

Enlightened minds have, since the 1730s, tried to demonstrate that deaths of this nature were due to an epidemic.[2] Jean Christophe Harenberg maintained "that vampires do not cause the death of the living, and everything that people reel off in this regard should be attributed only to disorder in the sick person's imagination."[3] By picking up on the medical information and the description of the symptoms, researchers have come to a hypotheses on this illness: it was cholera—hence the ruddy complexion of the vampires—plague, or even rabies . . .[4]

The Identification of the Vampire

The Stranger

There are three ways to identify a vampire: The first is the appearance of a disquieting stranger. To discover who he is, people used a decoding grid to analyze his behavior. In central Europe the monster could be recognized by his lameness, his iron teeth, his inability to count higher than three, and from the trade he plied while still a living man: he was a butcher or a bootmaker. This man had a very ruddy complexion; among the Slavs the expression "red as a vampire" (*cervoni jak vesci*) designates a rubicund individual while "fat as a vampire" refers to a heavy man. These distinctive features make it possible to recognize the unknown vampire—that is, one who was not part of the village community, a foreigner. Interestingly, these characteristics correspond quite precisely to what René Girard calls the "victim-hood signs," which is to say, all the clues that push a community to make one individual a scapegoat when it is countering a scourge.

The Form Taken by Death

The second way to identify a vampire plays out during a death. When there are doubts concerning the good death of a person, appeal is made to an expert, customarily a midwife, to examine the body of the deceased, and she equips herself with all that is necessary to ensure that the dead individual does not come back. In Greece an *alaphostratos*—a man endowed with second sight who was capable of seeing spirits and therefore of knowing if a body was really in the grave—accompanied the Orthodox priest. The suspicion of the living is aroused by unmistakable signs: the body remains limber and red, and its eyes remain open or half-closed. In 1748 a farmhand named Gloswatsch died in Lonkau, Upper Silesia; the next day his body was still not rigid. He returned and tormented and harried the other maids and servants there. The counselor to Parliament and the doctor could not uproot the beliefs of the folk of this area.[5] In 1779 a Silesian newspaper reported how a man had gone to a house where a death had recently taken place. He found the family in a state of high anxiety and eventually learned that someone else in the household would die in the very near future because the body had never become rigid.[6]

The motif of the open eyes is skillfully exploited by Bram Stoker. When Jonathan Harker finds Count Dracula's coffin, he notes:

> There, in one of the great boxes, of which there were fifty in all, on a pile of new freshly dug earth, lay the Count! He was either dead or asleep, I could not say which for his eyes were open and stony, but without the glassiness of death, and the cheeks had the warmth of life through all their pallor. The lips were as red as ever. But there was no sign of movement, no pulse, no breath, no beating of the heart.

When Carmilla's tomb is opened in Le Fanu's work, her body possesses all the appearance of life, as we can see in the extract in chapter 1.

The Opening of the Crypt

The third method of identification can be considered once it has become a certainty that a vampire is active in the region. This method consists of two major steps: the identification of the grave that shelters this creature—indispensable if you want to be able to take action—and the use of radical means of destruction. In the modern myth these two moments provide the climax of the stories and take place in remote and disquieting places, those made popular by cinema: a deconsecrated cemetery, an abandoned house, the crypt of a chapel in ruins—but all this is mere literature. The tales from earlier times tell us that this method occurred in places known to all and within the topography of the village.

Let's look at Théophile Gautier's novella: Romuald and the priest Serapion visit the cemetery where Clarimonde is buried. In the middle of the night, by the light provided by a dark lantern they eventually find:

> . . . a great slab, half concealed by huge weeds and devoured by mosses and parasitic plants . . . The owls, which had been nestling in the cypress-trees, startled by the gleam of the lantern, flew against it from time to time, striking their dusty wings against its panes, and uttering plaintive cries of lamentation. . . . At last Sérapion's

mattock struck the coffin itself, making its planks re-echo with a deep sonorous sound, with that terrible sound nothingness utters when stricken. He wrenched apart and tore up the lid, and I beheld Clarimonde, pallid as a figure of marble, with hands joined; her white winding-sheet made but one fold from her head to her feet. A little crimson drop sparkled like a speck of dew at one corner of her colourless mouth.

We can note the author's delicacy here: unlike Carmilla in the grave, Clarimonde is not lying in a bath of blood; she does not even have any color. Carmilla—not Clarimonde—deserves the name "the living dead." Each writer treats the scene with his own sensibility, but Théophile Gautier takes his distance from the ancient testimonies on this point and reports nothing that might be considered shocking. In fact, the tranquil beauty of his Clarimonde is rather moving.

In central Europe the final resting place of a vampire was recognizable because it had a hole through which he left and entered or because it was the landing site for falling stars. The following experiment was truly spectacular: the villagers gathered in the cemetery, where a white or black stallion, bull, or gander had to stride over all the graves. If the animal refused to cross any one of them, that grave was certain to contain a vampire who must be slain. In Wallachia "a young boy is chosen to ride entirely naked on a totally black horse, and the horse and boy are led to the cemetery. There they walk across all the graves. The one the animal refuses to cross over, even when hit by the crop, is regarded as containing a vampire." According to Captain L. de Beloz, in Hungary, there could be seen on this grave "a gleam similar to that of a lamp, but less bright."[7]

In other countries the distinctive signs of these suspect tombs were contradictory: in one place, it was declared that the earth would not subside or fall in on a suspect grave, whereas in another country, a suspect dead person had left a diametrically opposing sign.

In the seventeenth and eighteenth centuries, the expert was the gravedigger, because his métier enabled him to distinguish the "normal" dead from those who were far from it. One gravedigger, Hans Bürgel, was questioned on August 5, 1665, by the authorities of Michelsdorf of the earldom of Glaz in Silesia, who asked him three questions: "How and by what signs is it possible to know if these bodies are not correct? How did he know beforehand which tombs to open? Couldn't the same thing happen to the bodies of unsuspected individuals?" Here is Bürgel's response as preserved in the city archives of Wroclaw (Breslau):

> He answered the first question by saying that they were recognizable because of the pool of blood around them, the new skin that had grown over the old, and the nails that had grown beneath the old ones.
>
> To the second question he responded that he owned a plant that allowed him to recognize every suspect grave when he ate it. But he could also recognize them when he went to the cemetery without eating it. He revealed no more about this matter. . . .
>
> The third question he answered by saying it was impossible for normal bodies to be lying in a pool of blood and to have new skin and nails, because they decomposed. . . .
>
> He also stated that there was a difference between the seven bodies that had been exhumed: four possessed spirits so strong that it was not possible to master them immediately; the spirit of another corpse was of average strength, and that of the last two cadavers was quite weak; these last three individuals must have been led astray, shortly before their deaths, by frivolous folk and had not bespelled anyone.

What Hans Bürgel means by *spirit* remains vague today, but this was not the case at all in earlier times. The term in fact designates the aptitude to pursue a certain form of life. He notes the presence of something in the cadaver—anima, animus, or spiritus. It was this force that prevented the body from rotting. We should note here that this force was the same one that prevented the decomposition of the bodies of certain saints, as odd as this comparison may seem. In the legend of St. Quirin, as recorded on the table of a chapel dedicated to him in the Bavarian monastery of Tergernsee, the lines of this verse appear:

Three Bishops of Holy Law
and many priests
have, with reverence,
placed in this coffin
Saint Quirin, the patron saint.
When a priest named Rimbert
touched him, immediately
from the gentle body
a large quantity of blood
swiftly streamed out
as we see it still in the monstrance.[8]

In a different context, if there had been an epidemic or a series of suspicious deaths, how would this bloodshed be interpreted if not as the sign of vampirism? This example underscores the importance of the circumstances in which such events unfurl. Yet Quirin had been made a martyr at the hands of the emperor Claudius. He died so that the true faith would triumph; his death therefore does not put him into the category of wicked dead who seek vengeance from beyond the grave. Consequntly, the fluidity of his blood was a divine miracle and not diabolical.

Sorcerers and witches were predisposed to turn into vampires, but, fortunately, there were certain signs by which they could be recognized: a wine-colored birthmark on the foot, a chisel/scissors in the back, being born with long teeth, having one tooth that stuck out in front of the others, or having a double row of teeth. Presumed vampires were also recognizable by a harelip or the absence of a nose.

Another infallible method of identification was the nudity of the body that was exhumed. In 1572 the tomb of a woman in Rhezur, Poland, was opened and it was observed that she was naked, from which it was concluded that she had eaten her grave clothes.[9] There is another detail that caused much ink to flow during the eighteenth century. The official reports alluded to it without spelling out reasons that could be easily grasped: the penis was erect on a male vampire's corpse.

Of course, the novelists never dare help themselves to this detail for reasons of propriety. Scholars such as Michaël Ranft, however, have examined this detail closely and have advanced physical and medical reasons: "The penis, which is spongy by nature, can spontaneously rise on the corpse as a fluid or breath enters the hypogastric artery."[10] Of course, however, this erect penis is proof positive that these out-of-the-ordinary dead men possess sexual impulses that compel them to attack women, and we have already seen cases in which revenants desired sexual relations with their widows. Appendix 1 contains additional documentary evidence. There is a final detail that will fool no one: beard, hair, skin, and nails were interpreted before as the certain sign of the vegetative life of the corpse. Sometimes it was even claimed that the palms of vampires were covered with hair, a means of emphasizing their otherness.

The modern myth, thanks to Le Fanu, introduced a new element: a singular dentition. When the mountebank catches sight of the heroine of the story and Carmilla at the window of the castle, he notes the vampire's teeth and says: "Your noble friend, the young lady at your right, has the sharpest tooth—long, thin, pointed, like an awl, like a needle." And in Bram Stoker's novel, Jonathan Harker notes in his description of Dracula: "The count . . . drew back. And with a grim sort of smile, which showed more than he had yet done his protuberant teeth." Further, the three vampire women who surprise him while he is sleeping on a couch have "brilliant white teeth that shone like pearls against the ruby of their voluptuous lips." Finally, we can all recall the actor Christopher Lee sporting two canine teeth of respectable size in the films based in part on Bram Stoker's novel.

There is another means of identification that was introduced by the novelists of the nineteenth century: the absence of the body in its coffin when the grave is opened at night. This is a decisive moment in Bram Stoker's book, and the proof is revealed when Lucy Westenra is a vampire. Abraham van Helsing goes to the cemetery with Dr. Seward, Lucy's fiancé, Arthur, and Quincey Morris, and they all enter the crypt.

He [van Helsing] took his screwdriver and again took off the lid of the coffin. Arthur looked on, very pale but silent. When the lid was removed he stepped forward. He evidently did not know there was a leaden coffin, or at any rate, had not thought of it. When he saw the rent in the lead, the blood rushed to his face for an instant, but as quickly fell away again, so that he remained a ghastly white. He was still silent. Van Helsing forced back the leaden flange, and we all looked in and recoiled.

The coffin was empty!

The Execution of the Vampire

The destruction of the vampire remains the peak of horror and fright in Gothic novels and movies. In *Clarimonde,* Théophile Gautier is able to re-create admirably the ambience that prevails at this moment. Yet there is no happy ending in Alexei Tolstoy's book: the hero escapes the family of vampires but does not eliminate them. For his part Sheridan Le Fanu prepares and conditions his readers for the final scene by bringing a forest ranger into the moment: "'How came the village to be deserted' asked the General. 'It was troubled by *revenants,* sir, several were tracked to their graves, there detected by the usual tests, and extinguished in the usual ways, by decapitation, by the stake, and by burning.'"

The man then tells them a story, for which we have several variations, from the eighteenth century.

> "But after all these proceedings according to law," he continued, "so many graves opened, and so many vampires deprived of their horrible animation—the village was not relieved. But a Moravian nobleman, who happened to be traveling this way, heard how matters were, and being skilled—as many people are in his country—in such affairs, he offered to deliver the village from its tormentor. He did so thus: There being a bright moon that night, he ascended, shortly after sunset, the towers of the chapel here, from whence he could distinctly see the churchyard beneath him; you can see it from that window.

From this point he watched until he saw the vampire come out of his grave, and place near it the linen clothes in which he had been folded, and then glide away toward the village to plague its inhabitants."

The stranger, having seen all this, comes down from the steeple, takes the linen wrappings of the vampire, and carries them up to the top of the tower, which he again mounts. When the vampire returns from his prowlings and misses his clothes, he cries furiously to the Moravian, whom he sees at the summit of the tower, and who, in reply, beckons him to ascend and take them. The vampire, accepting this invitation, begins to climb the steeple, and as soon as he reaches the battlements, the Moravian, with a stroke of his sword, cleaves his skull in two, hurling him down to the churchyard. Descending by the winding stairs, the stranger follows and cuts off his head. The next day, he delivers it and the body to the villagers, who duly impale and burn them.

This story is based on an event that took place in the Moravian town of Egwanschitz around 1617. The vampire there was killed with a blow from a spade, then chopped into pieces. The accent on the legality of the procedure is sure to catch our attention. It is borrowed from the "reality" of the exhumations of Silesian, Hungarian, and Serbian vampires during the previous century. The profanation of tombs was not a matter to be treated lightly; everything had to be done according to form and with the consent of the local authorities. Le Fanu mentions it again when Carmilla's tomb is opened: "The next day the formal proceedings took place in the Chapel of Karnstein," and the heroine of the story declares: "My father has a copy of the report of the Imperial Commission, with the signatures of all who were present at these proceedings, attached in verification of the statement. It is from this official paper that I have summarized my account of this last shocking scene."

One recurring detail does, however, remain mysterious: Why are the vampires obliged to leave behind their shrouds on their graves? One hypothesis is that the shroud is the mark of their new status as the dead. When they leave to attack the living, they are transgressing this status, and the shroud perhaps represents the bond that connects them to the grave—unless it is merely a fiction intended to facilitate their elimination. The theft of this garment causes them to fall into a trap and lose what remains of their life.

We witness two vampire slayings in Bram Stoker's novel. Dracula is killed when he is stabbed directly in the heart by a bowie knife: "It was like a miracle, but before our very eyes, and almost in the drawing of a breath, the whole body crumbled into dust and passed from our sight." Time reclaims its rights and does its work. The staging of the death of Lucy, his victim, is remarkable.

> Arthur took the stake and the hammer, and when once his mind was set on action his hands never trembled nor even quivered. Van Helsing opened his missal and began to read, and Quincey and I followed as well as we could. Arthur placed the point over the heart, and as I looked I could see its dint in the white flesh. Then he struck with all his might.
>
> The thing in the coffin writhed, and a hideous, blood-curdling screech came from the opened red lips. The body shook and quivered and twisted in wild contortions. The sharp white teeth champed together till the lips were cut, and the mouth was smeared with a crimson foam. But Arthur never faltered. He looked like a figure of Thor as his untrembling arm rose and fell, driving deeper and deeper the mercy-bearing stake, whilst the blood from the pierced heart welled and spurted up around it.

To determine the contribution of the writers, it is necessary to be able to compare what they say to what their ancestors recorded. The most ancient retelling of the execution of a vampire, then called a *sanguisuga* [bloodsucker], can be read in the *Chronicle* of William of Newbury (1136–1198). In it a cuckold returns after his death although he did receive a Christian burial.

> [He] was soon seen during the hours of night: to come forth from

his tomb and wander about all through the streets, prowling round the houses whilst on every side the dogs were howling and yelping the whole night long. Throughout the whole district then every man locked and barred his door, nor did anyone between the hours of dusk and dawn dare go out on any business whatsoever. Yet even these precautions were of no avail, for the air became foul and tainted as this fetid and corrupting body wandered abroad, so that a terrible plague broke out and there was hardly a house that did not mourn its dead. The parish priest, the good man from whose mouth I learned this story, was grieved to the heart at this trouble, which had fallen upon his flock. Accordingly upon Palm Sunday he called together a number of wise and devout men who might advise him what was the best course to take.

While they were gathered over a meal two young men who had lost their father to the plague and were afraid for their own lives decided to take matters into their own hands: They armed themselves, therefore, with sharp spades and, betaking themselves to the cemetery, they began to dig. And whilst they yet thought they would have to dig much deeper, suddenly they came upon the body covered with but a thin layer of earth. It was gorged and swollen with a frightful corpulence. Its face was florid and chubby, with huge red puffed cheeks, and the shroud in which he had been wrapped was all soiled and torn. But the young men, who were mad with grief and anger, were not in any way frightened. They at once dealt the corpse a sharp blow with the keen edge of a spade and immediately there gushed out such a stream of warm red gore that they realized this sanguisuga had battened in the blood of many poor folk. Accordingly they dragged it outside the town and here they quickly built a large pyre. One of them having said that a corpse carrying the plague could not be burned as long as the heart had not been removed, the other slashed open the side of the body with repeated blows from his blunt hoe, plunged in his hand, and tore out the cursed heart, which was cut into pieces on the spot. . . . Now, no sooner had that infernal monster been thus destroyed than the plague entirely ceased, just as if the polluted air was cleansed by the fire which burned up the hellish brute who had infected the whole atmosphere.[11]

We can note that the execution of the dead man included the extraction of the heart considered as the "motor" of the body. If this had not been done, it would have proved impossible to incinerate the body. This means of proceeding is but one among a host of others. We find it mentioned again around 1919–1920 in Bucovina (northern Romania), where the following took place: A series of deaths near Cusmir occurred in the same family. Suspicions fell upon an old man who was already long dead. When he was exhumed, he was found squatting and completely rosy, for he had actually devoured his entire family, many of whom were sturdy young men in the best of health. When an attempt was made to remove him from the grave, he resisted. It was horrible and terrible. Someone gave him a blow with an ax and pulled him from the grave, but it proved impossible to slice into his body with a knife. A sickle and a large ax were then used. His heart and liver were removed and burned, then the ashes were mixed with water and given to the sick to drink. They drank the mixture and recovered. The old man was reburied and no one else died.[12]

Among the measures taken to get rid of presumed vampires, measures that are not the stuff of novels but correspond to the reality of the narrators, the dismemberment of the corpse has been mentioned frequently since 1592 (see appendix 3) and did not vanish until the beginning of the twentieth century. We may judge how prevalent it was from this Romanian testimony:

Around fifteen years ago, the old mother of the peasant Dinu Georghita died in the village of Amarasti, north of Dolj. Several months later, her son's children began dying one after the other, then it became the turn of the children of his younger brother. Her sons grew frightened and opened the grave one night, cut the body in half, and put it back in place. Despite this, the deaths did not cease—far from it. They therefore opened the grave again and what did they find? The cadaver was intact without a single wound! It was a great marvel. They took it out of the grave and carried it into the forest, where they placed it in a remote corner of the woods. There they opened the body, removed the heart, from which blood flowed, cut it into four pieces, and cast it into a charcoal fire and burned it. They collected the ashes, mixed them with water, and gave it to their children to drink. They cast the cadaver into the flames, incinerating it, then buried the ashes. The deaths came to an end.[13]

In the modern myth, we encounter other means of elimination. The most "gentle" is still the blessing of the corpse once the sepulchre has been opened. "And he [Sérapion]," writes Théophile Gautier, "flung holy water upon the corpse and the coffin, over which he traced the sign of the cross with his sprinkler. Poor Clarimonde had no sooner been touched by the blessed spray than her beautiful body crumbled into dust, and became only a shapeless and frightful mass of cinders and half-calcined bones." This is not merely literature! Collin de Plancy and Dom Calmet cite the case of a Greek vampire who dissolved the very moment the patriarch made the sign of absolution. In a Russian tale collected by Afanassiev, the vampire passes away when someone says: "God cause you to die!"[14] The assistance of religion is not an absolute necessity: in a village near Gdansk, a vampire crumbled into dust with a death rattle when he was decapitated.

We should also not believe that impalement is the prerogative of vampires alone. It can be applied to any dead individual whose return is particularly dreaded. In the Belgian hamlet of Tergnée, near Gilly, excavations performed in a chapel unearthed five coffins, each pierced through with a large nail at the level of the chest. They belonged to the lords of Faciennes, buried during the middle of the eighteenth century: Count Charles-Joseph de Batthyany; his wife, Anne de Waldstein, daughter of a Bohemian landgrave; and their children, who died of languor.[15] These deaths were eminently suspect and justified the precautions that were taken.

The modern myth has elected Romania to be land of vampires— but let's examine what local beliefs have left us, particularly beliefs concerning the murony. If a deceased individual was suspected of being one, a long needle was buried in his skull; the body was daubed with the lard of a pig slaughtered on the day of St. Ignatius, five days before Christmas; and a thorn-covered wild rose plant the length of a stocking was set on top of it, which would prevent it from leaving its tomb, because its shroud would get tangled in it.

To slay it, appeal was made to a specialist killer: a foreigner, Muslim, a Gypsy, a man born on Saturday, or the son of a vampire. In Bram Stoker's book, the Gypsies are Dracula's auxiliary troops, and they seem to harbor no dread of him whatsoever. In Romania the deceased was dug up and a man born on Saturday buried a garlic-smeared stake in the corpse's heart. The dead then uttered heartrending cries and blood as black as coal tar spurted from his heart—then the heart was cooked in wine and pierced with a needle. Sometimes the body was dismembered and thrown to wild animals or burned or only the heart was burned or the heart was burned with the liver. Wealthy families sprinkled the body with wine and put it back into the ground with its face turned down. Finally, a rooster was interred on the grave—its song sends spirits fleeing—to keep the dead person from coming back. In Morea [on the Peloponnesian peninsula of Greece], the broucalaca were dismembered then boiled in wine.

We should especially refrain from thinking that the execution of a vampire is a simple matter: these bloodsuckers have their souls nailed to their bodies! In the fourteenth century Mysslata, a shepherd from the Bohemian village of Cadan, was suspected of being a vampire, and his elimination gave rise to stupefying manifestations that Charles Ferdinand von Schertz recorded in his treatise *Magia Posthuma*.

> To put an end to their woes, the inhabitants of this village and the surrounding area gathered together, deliberated, then had the body disinterred, whereupon it was impaled upon an oak stake, but he [the vampire] only laughed—he, or his ghost rather, because in Hell he would not have such an urge to laugh—and said: "You think you have played a fine trick on me, but all you have done is given me a fine staff the better to defend myself with against the dogs!" And he came

back the next night and harried folk worse than before. He was given to the hangman who took him on a cart outside the village to burn him. The corpse shouted like a mad man, moved his feet as if still alive, and when he was once again pierced through with the stake, he howled and spilled a large quantity of beautifully deep red blood. He was finally reduced to ashes and never again appeared to attack folk.

A splendid testimony! Because the exhumed body shouts and moves, scholars have advanced simple and lucid explanations: "The air that was sealed inside the cadaver, and then violently released necessarily produced this noise while passing through the throat" when the heart was pierced with a stake. Yet they failed to convince the common man—far from it! According to another document, the corpse of Martin Weimar, a wizard from the Landeshut region, was treated this way in 1671: He was disinterred and his hands were bound behind his back, for this rendered him helpless. He was then decapitated and burned to ashes and his tomb was walled up.[16]

We possess a good piece of "reporting" on a case of vampirism, in which ancestral measures work hand in hand with Christian practices. The dead man is a knocker, an eater, and a fornicator.

In 1672 this locale—the market town of Krinck—expirenced an extraordinary event: the body of a dead man named Giure (Georg) Grando was dug up then, in a distinctive ritual, his head was cut off so he would leave folk in peace. In fact, following the decease of said individual, once he had been buried in conformance with Christian custom, he was seen wandering about this town the night following his burial. He started by showing himself to Father George, a monk of St. Paul the Hermit, who had said his funeral Mass and presided over his interment. When this monk sought to return home after the funeral feast at the widow's house with friends of the deceased, he saw the dead man sitting behind the door and he left in terror. Grando next appeared to a number of his friends at night when he strolled through the streets and knocked on the doors of houses, sometimes here and sometimes there, after which different people died. In fact, soon emerging from those dwellings on whose doors he had rapped, were dead persons. He had also made his way to his widow's house, actually slept with her, and she, horrified, finally went to see the local bailiff Miho Radetich, where she begged him to procure aid against her late husband. The bailiff therefore summoned several courageous neighbors, gave them strong spirits to drink, and convinced them to lend aid to the widow and bring an end to this scourge as Guire or Georg Grando had already devoured some of her neighbors and molested his wife every night. They decided to attack the night stalker and chill his desire to come out. According to the bailiff, they were nine in number with two lanterns and a crucifix when they opened the grave. They then discovered that the cadaver's face was flushed red; he turned and looked at them with a smile, then opened his mouth. These bellicose ghost slayers were so terrified that they all fled as one man. The bailiff was quite irritated to see that nine living men were incapable of handling a dead man and were transformed into scared rabbits by a single glance. He scolded them and urged them to return once more to the tomb and try to pierce the [dead man's] belly with a sharp hawthorn stake. But the stakes only bounced back off every time. In the meantime, the bailiff had summoned a priest who showed a crucifix to the dead man and told him: "Look at this Strigon! Here is Jesus Christ who delivered us from the pains of hell and died for us. And you, strigon, you cannot find rest," and so forth. And this exorcist or necromancer* said many other similar things. Tears then fell from the eyes of the corpses. However, as it was impossible to impale his body, Micolo Nyena, an inhabitant of Mehrenfelss, tried to cut off his head with a hoe, but because he was too fearful and went about it too timidly, the more valiant provost-marshal, Milasich, stepped in and sent the dead man's head flying. At that moment, the latter let out a shriek as if he were still alive and he filled his grave with blood. After having

---

*The text uses the word *Todten*, which equates with *Redner*, "he who speaks to the dead."

done this, the noble executioners returned home and, henceforth, Grando left his wife and other folk in peace.[17]

In reading the different reports on the dispatching *ad patres* of vampires, we can see that they attest only to the perennial nature of beliefs and ancient measures applied to simple revenants. Because these individuals were the subject of study in another book of mine,[18] I will content myself with referring to the example of a particularly tough and obstinate dead man, noting that in this bygone era, getting rid of a dead person was no easy task. Spade, ax, and sword certainly could injure him, but he recovered quickly from the damage they inflicted. Only cremation followed by immersion of the ashes in running water had a definitive effect. We can refer to Thorolf Twist-Foot, who lived around the year 1000. A wicked man, he did not rest in peace. Once night fell, it was not a good idea for the living to be caught outside. Livestock that came too near his tomb died and any bird who flew over it perished. Thorolf murdered a shepherd who was found with every bone in his body broken. He haunted the common room of his former domicile, attacking everyone and sending all fleeing for their lives. Then, he and everyone he had killed formed a band. He was exhumed so that he could be buried farther away, far away from man and beast, and hauling his corpse to its new home was difficult: it was both hideous and enormous. Thorolf continued committing criminal acts, and he was disinterred again and burned. Another revenant, Klaufi, whose behavior was similar, was dug up, and those exhuming him found his body had not decomposed. He was burned and his ashes were placed in a lead casket sealed by two iron hooks. The ashes were then tossed into a spring.[19]

The execution of vampires was entirely ritualized: every stage of the process occured in accordance with a procedure well anchored in reality. The authorities from whom aid and protection were asked were invited to intervene. They authorized the exhumation and designated the executioners, sometimes accompanying them personally or sending proxies. When the traditional measures appeared to fail, a priest was summoned, but sometimes events occurred in the reverse order, which testifies to a certain reluctance to mutilate a corpse, an action long considered a crime by the legislature. Killing a vampire was a legal act that was sometimes preceded by a trial in which the dead individual was accused of causing disorder or murder. The court heard witnesses, but there is no trace of any lawyer for the defense in the documents I have scrutinized, and sometimes the family mounted a ferocious opposition to the disinterment or else lodged an appeal, as happened in 1801. Marguna Warlin was presumed to be a witch a and was recognized as such by the presence, it was claimed, of shears in her back. She was buried on her stomach after dirt had been placed in her nose and a Ticket of St. Luke was placed in her mouth. Her daughter filed a complaint, and the parish priest of Gross-Gorschütz had the body exhumed. Because no scissors were found, the dirt from her nose and the ticket were removed, and she was given a Christian burial on May 15 in the presence of the village tribunal.[20]

If the case had been judged and the dead was found guilty—often under the pressure of the inhabitants, who threatened to leave or carry out their own justice—an executioner was summoned, and if there was not one in the area, one was brought in from outside or a local was appointed to fulfill that office. Depending on the time and place, the performance of the execution was more or less "barbaric," as we have seen.

Long before Maria Teresa issued her ban on executing the dead in 1755, a procedure had been put in place. In 1667 four dead women were deemed to be responsible for the deaths of twenty people in a market town to the north of Neisse, in Silesia. On May 9 the municipal doctor, Christoph Geller, examined the disinterred bodies in the company of a barber by the name of Caspar Lübecken and found them suspicious "because of the presence of fresh blood." To learn what should be done, he contacted the bishop of Breslau, who ordered the town council to perform additional tests, none of which provided convincing results, and the bodies were reburied.[21]

Here is the testimony of Milord de Cabreras in 1730. After having encountered a revenant in the house of a Hungarian where he was staying:

... [a] soldier informed the others in his regiment, who passed it on to the general officers, who then contacted the Count de Cabreras, the captain of the Alandetti infantry, to check out the facts. Going to the site of the event with a surgeon, an auditor, and some of his fellow officers, he took the depositions of the entire household, who confirmed unanimously that the revenant was the father of the master of the house, and that everything the soldier had said and reported was the pure unvarnished truth; statements immediately confirmed by all the village inhabitants. Consequently, the body of this specter was then ordered exhumed and his body was discovered to be like that of someone who had just died and his blood was like that of a living man. The Count de Cabreras had him decapitated and put back in his grave. He then asked if there were other similar creatures and was told of several, among them a man who had died more than thirty years previously. He had returned to his former home on three occasions, always at mealtime. The first time he sucked the blood from the neck of his own brother, the second one of his sons, and the third time one of the servants—all three died on the spot. Based on this deposition, the count ordered this man pulled from the earth and he was found in a similar state as the first with his blood flowing as if he were a living man. He ordered a nail driven into the head of this individual and the body was then put back into the grave. He had a third body burned, that of someone who had died sixteen years earlier and had returned to suck the blood and cause the death of his sons. The commissioner sent in his report to the general officers who forwarded it on to the Court of the Emperor, who commanded that military and legal authorities be sent along with doctors, surgeons, and several scholars to examine the causes of these events.[22]

All of this had to be done with the strictest legality and with complete respect for the taboos of the church. Pope Boniface VIII promulgated a law Against the Detestable Exhumations of Graves, and there are numerous judicial texts, starting from the early Middle Ages, that deal with the punishment of tomb profaners. Rather than disinterring suspicious dead, it was preferred to delay their burial. "Sometimes burial of the bodies of suspect individuals is deferred for six or seven weeks. When they do not decay and their limbs remain flexible and workable, as if they were alive, then they are burned."[23]

We must avoid assuming that such actions are all confined to a remote past. In 1874 an inhabitant of Rhode Island exhumed the body of his daughter and burned her heart in the belief she was threatening the lives of other family members. During this same time another woman, who died of tuberculosis, suffered a similar fate, but in this instance it was her lungs that were incinerated. In 1899 peasants from Krassowa, in Romania, dug up about thirty corpses and dismembered them in order to bring an end to an epidemic of diphtheria, and in 1912 a Hungarian farmer who had been attacked by ghosts went to the cemetery, placed three large cloves of garlic in the corpse and three stones in its mouth, and then nailed it to the ground by impaling it with a stake.[24] These are only a few examples from a body of documents that consists of a hundred such cases from just the nineteenth and twentieth centuries! These few examples should be enough to satisfy us, for the testimonies, accounts, and other reports are very repetitive. Their sole value is that they allow us to map out the spread of the belief, its expansion, and its focal points.

From the anthropological point of view, the slaying of the vampire can be incorporated perfectly into what René Girard calls "a collective murder,"[25] and it corresponds exactly to the outline he extracted from the myth of Oedipus.

1. A scourge attacks a community.
2. To put an end to it, the community seeks the responsible party. Tongues are loosened and people recall facts that initially appeared harmless, which added together confirm the suspicions people have about a dead person.
3. A list is made of "the signs of victimhood," which, in the vampire myth, are connected to the physical appearance of the deceased, the day and hour of his the vampire's birth, or even the vampire's

trade—in short, everything that contributed to making the dead individual a marginal member of the community.

4. The entire community takes part in the execution through the intermediary of a representative—a hangman or executioner designated by the municipal officials.

The sequence of events in this procedure that transforms a dead person into a scapegoat is similar in every detail to the one involved in lodging an accusation of witchcraft. Confronted by a scourge, the human community bonds to eliminate the troublemaker collectively. In short, it exorcises the evil and eradicates the tumor from its midst. In the documents I've examined, the pressure of the *vox populi* is cited on more than one occasion, and the authorities are compelled to bow to it if they do not want to see the area deserted. Everything takes place as if the community had to commit a collective murder at regular intervals and had to purge itself of its defects and anxieties by designating a victim in its midst. It is specifically this aspect that René Girard has been able to distinguish clearly in so many myths. It explains why the vampire epidemic rose when the last fires burning the witches were extinguished, which is something we will revisit. It also sheds light on the survival of vampires in novels and the cinema.

How to Cure the Bite of a Vampire

The bite of a vampire entails a loss of blood that leads to death. Bram Stoker exploits this to the fullest and shows us Lucy Westenra being kept alive through repeated blood transfusions, but Count Dracula finally wins out. Generally the victim cannot recover until the vampire is destroyed: "It was cast back into the grave with lots of quicklime to hasten its consumption," de Beloz states, concerning an executed vampire, "and since then, his niece, who had been sucked twice, was doing better."[26] Abraham van Helsing, speaking of Lucy's victims, says: "Those children whose blood she sucked are not as yet so much the worse, but if she lives on, UnDead, more and more they lose their blood and by her power over them they come to her, and so she draw their blood with that so wicked mouth. But if she die in truth, then all cease. The tiny wounds of the throats disappear . . ." All Stoker does is draw the lessons provided by the old testimonies and recasts them in a poignant literary form.

The documents from our corpus propose other fairly distasteful measures of protection: The relatives inhaled the smoke of the body as it was incinerated. An individual could also ingest a blend made from vampire ashes or resulting from the cremation of the heart and the liver or—what a paradox—can reverse roles and drink the vampire's blood. Around 1750 this medicine was used in eastern Prussia. We have a notable retelling of an event that suggests it without saying it outright. This can mean one of two things: either everyone understood and there was no need to spell it out, or the fact was concealed because it was regarded as reprehensible.

During the middle of the last century, a member of the noble Wollschläger family died in western Prussia. Several of his kin unexpectedly followed him to the grave soon after with no clear cause for their demise. It was immediately recalled that the face of the dead man had not lost its ruddy complexion, which convinced people of his vampire nature. A family council was held and it was decided that Joseph von Wollschäger would decapitate his late uncle. At this time Joseph, who died in 1820 at an advanced age as governor of the district, was still a young man. Accompanied by a monk from the Benedictine Cloister of Jacobsdorf, each of them holding a candle, they descended into the crypt of the monastery where the deceased was interred.

They opened the coffin and pulled out the body so that its neck was resting on the edge of the casket. The natural movement the head made by lolling backward inspired such terror in the monk that he dropped his candle and took flight. Although now alone, Joseph von Wollschäger did not faint and separated the head from the body with the ax he had brought with him, but a powerful stream of blood sprung out at this contact and extinguished the last candle. In almost total darkness, he managed to collect up a little of the blood in a metal goblet and returned home with it. This action intended to preserve the lives of his family almost cost him his own; he was stricken with a dangerous illness that kept him on the edge of the grave for six months. One can still see today, in the crypt of the Jacobsdorf cloister, exactly inside the middle chamber where the Wollschläger cellar is located, a body with its head between its feet.[27]

Why go to the trouble of collecting the blood in a drinking vessel if not for the purpose of giving it to one or more people suffering from a mysterious condition?

Another report confirms this prophylactic measure. The steward of Count Simon Mabiensku, staroste of Posnania, died and was buried, but after some suspect manifestations in his crypt, the corpse was hauled out of the tomb so that its head could be cut off. The dead man ground his teeth, and a healthy flow of blood poured from the body. A white handkerchief was dipped into the dead man's blood and the entire household was made to drink some of it so as to spare them torment. Another method involved eating bread made from the blood that had spilled from a vampire's corpse, which Dom Calmet condemns, because he views it as one evil spell taking the place of another,[28] an opinion echoed by another Parisian doctor, who notes:

> It seems that permission should not be given to open graves, to cutting off the head, to opening the heart of a dead person, to collecting the blood from his body so that bread can be made from it or it be drunk, nor that anyone be allowed to do any of those things just mentioned for whatever reason or pretext. It seems that these are evil and superstitious practices that have been invented and taught by the demon and have in themselves no virtue or any effectiveness in reducing or eliminating similar demonic persecution.[29]

Here is a passage that strongly reveals the mind-set of a bygone age. We can note the use of the verb *to seem,* a fine expression of the disarray that struck the enlightened minds of the eighteenth century at the sight of such strange and terrifying displays.

8

Questions and Answers

Press thy mouth against my mouth
Human's breath is divine!
I am drinking up your soul
The dead are insatiable . . .*

HEINRICH HEINE

THE VAMPIRE HAS inspired a thousand questions to which the men of an older era supplied several answers. He is a figure that is neither alive nor dead, haunting the steps of the beyond but resting close to men, capable of going out at day or night, combining within itself all the opposites—hate and love, good and evil, transgressing every norm, redeemer and author of damnation, "dark Christ who claims to give Life in death,"[1] an emanation of the forces of darkness, possessed by a monstrous thirst and hunger, inhabited by fear and the desire to die, dreading solitude.

---

*The words spoken by the beautiful Helena when Doctor Faust brings her back from the grave.

The Emergence of Vampirism

It is not by chance if, historically speaking, vampires flourished during the eighteenth century. Under the knife blows of Reason, religion retreated and its notion of life and death were called into question again. Science was the new dogma, and it was up to it to explain the workings of the world and rid it of the "rubbish of superstitions." Yet people continued to communicate in the ancient beliefs. We can see Emmanuel Swedenborg talking with the dead and the angels in 1743. These notions, attacked by the rationalists, failed to vanish because they gave structure to thought and carried a message of hope and consolation and justice—in short, they play an important role in society. The negation of transcendence was replaced by the religion of humanity, by the "utopia of a radiant future" characteristic of materialist doctrines.

During this time, medicine took a particularly keen interest in death and how to define it in order to avoid, among other things, the burial of people who were still alive but had fallen into cataleptic stupors and thereby showed all the clinical signs of death. A short treatise by Jacques Bénigne Vinslow appeared on the subject in 1742 in Paris, accompanied by the commentary of another doctor, Jacques-Jean Bruhier. To the scholars of that era, chewers, for example, were individuals who had been buried alive and that, in their despair, devoured their hands and shroud.

For other scholars such as Christian Frederic Garmann (1640–1708), who has left us an odd treatise in *De miraculis mortuorum* (The Wonders of the Dead), it was death itself and the dead body that were subjects of study, and his investigations led him to two major observations. Philippe Ariès has summed them up.

> In sleep and death the soul is concentrated outside the body instead of being distributed throughout it . . . The second theory, in conformance with scholastic philosophy, is that life is neither matter nor substance, it is the form: *ipsissima rei forma*. It is light and origin (*initium formale*), an origin that is always provided by the creator every time, like flint produces a spark.[2]

We will revisit these points again.

There is also another historical factor—which scholars such as Gábor Klaniczay and Karin Lambrecht have recently discovered—that has played an important role. The emergence of vampirism coincided with the end of the witch hunts in Europe, as if the people of this time needed to exorcise their terrors and needed an explanation for the evils—such as repeated epidemics of cholera and plague—that assailed them.[3] The meticulous comparison of the execution of witches to that of vampires reveals the same modus operandi and mind-set, and, with the help of Hungarian documents, Eva Pócs clearly demonstrates the role played by witch revenants after their deaths in the propagation of disease.[4]

Furthermore, the first accusation brought to bear against vampires was clearly that of sorcery. We have only to recall the title Charles Ferdinand von Schertz gave to his resounding treatise: *Posthumous Magic.* Vampires resembled the dead wizards whose pernicious activities remained unremarked during their lifetimes and whose true nature was displayed after their deaths. The telltale signs exhibited by their bodies were the same as those of the bloodsuckers. Here again, the explanations are starkly simple: the earth refused to receive them, and the devil had given them a singular kind of life by virtue of the pact they concluded with him while still alive. Proof of this can be seen when Christian measures taken against them proved effective—and if they were ineffective, it was a sign of the devil's great power, and the carrier of his malevolence was then destroyed by fire.

The transition from the repression of witchcraft to that of the elimination of vampirism is particularly clear-cut at the end of the sixteenth century. In 1572 in Lossen, near Brieg, a woman was exhumed: "On July 17, the peasants and the municipality have authorized the exhumation of a woman who had been a condemned witch and who died. She chewed so loudly in her grave that it could be heard far away. Her head was struck off with a spade and buried separately. She had devoured her shroud."[5]

We could also undoubtedly refer to an affair that had a huge impact throughout the Austro-Hungarian Empire during the turning point of the seventeenth and eighteenth centuries: Erzebeth Bathory, nicknamed the Bloody Countess, was a veritable human vampire who claimed to rejuvenate and regenerate herself by coating herself with the blood of the young women she tortured and slew in her castle of Csejthe in the district of Nyitra, in northwestern Hungary. It is said that one day in 1586 or 1587, a pale young man dressed in black arrived at this castle. He had black eyes and hair and long canines, so it was thought he was a vampire. He allegedly turned the countess into a vampire, which is one way of explaining this woman's monstrous behavior.[6] Here history mixes with legend, but it is easy to imagine that the results of the search of the castle led by Count Thurso and the parish priest of Csejthe on December 29, 1610, were well known to all and sundry and that tongues were long kept busy wagging in the thatched cottages of the entire region.

The Opinion of Theologians

For theologians, the vampire, who called into question body/soul dualism and was an offense against the laws of nature, was a sinner who died without remission—an excommunicate. His cadaver was therefore easy prey for demons, and it seemed to come back to life because they possessed and reanimated it. In Moldavia it was the evil spirit known as the *drakul* that was responsible for this phenomenon. From drakul to the vampire Dracula is only a step! The ecclesiastics and their flocks found proof of this explanation when they saw the corpse crumble into dust when it was absolved and blessed.

Possession is undoubtedly the oldest theory put forth by the church to explain the phenomenon, and from the twelfth century on we start encountering such phrases as: "The devil . . . animates his own container,[7] hence the use of the cross, the host, or holy water to send Satan fleeing." The knight Ricaut notes around 1740 "that the Greeks feel an evil spirit enters the body of those who died in a state of excommunication and that it prevents them from decaying by animating and moving them, a little like the way the soul animates and moves the body."[8] Yet the devil could take possession of the body and animate it because it had not been interred properly in accordance with Christian rites or because the body was that of an excommunicate, and the curse issued by the church concerning excommunicates is quite clear: "May wood, stone, and iron dissolve, but the excommunicates never!"[9] The vampire was such an individual: the otherworld rejected him and the earth refused to consume him. He was banned from the society of the dead and the society of the living, cursed for eternity, and his actions could be interpreted as motivated by vengeance.

The Age of Reason and the Enlightenment accepted the existence of spirits and the devil: "Sometimes, without doubt, the apparition can be produced independently of the individual, insofar as a spirit is probably capable of donning a fantasy body in the air."[10] We can find no notable progress through comparison to the Middle Ages. The ideas of the church still had the force of law, but all the same, it is surprising to read in 1728:

> We shall not contest that the devil may sometimes lurk in cemeteries, invested with a substantial power, but this does not happen very often because, as often thought, God seeks to preserve the tombs of pious persons and keep them unscathed by the malice and wicked jokes of the Devil. Therefore, in those places where murders or massacres were committed, we do not deny that specters can be seen, and that various tumults and doleful noises, words of lamentations or moans, may be heard . . .[11]

The activity of the devil, a veritable deus ex machina with a broad back, helps justify the existence of ghosts, revenants, and *poltergeister,* and there was a clear distinction bewveen the manner of death of the just-departed and that of sinners. Here we find again the primary and fundamental distinction between the gallant deceased and the wicked dead, between the good death and the bad death. In 1610 a suspect cadaver was entrusted to the keeping of the pastor who stated that "the devil's presence is extremely strong in this body," and at the request of the dead person's own children, it was incinerated on May 6.[12] Even in 1728 it was imagined in scholarly and clerical circles that the dead could seek vengeance. Ranft states that there are no grounds for surprise that Peter Plogojovitz killed nine people after his death. "Perhaps he had such fierce quarrels with these neighbors that he could not even find rest in death."[13] What emerges from all this is that today as yesterday people believe that the dead still hold on to enough life to act simply if there is a strong reason preventing them from finding peace.

The Opinion of the Medical Profession

For scholars, doctors, and physiologists, the vampire is only a corpse that holds life, a vegetative force—*vis vegetative*—proof for which can be found in the growth of the nails, hair, and even skin. The absence of decay in certain disinterred cadavers, regarded by the "little people" as proof the dead person is a vampire, is explained, say those in the medical profession, by the nature of the place in which they were buried. The examples they cite are those that all can verify: the fluidity of the blood, the ruddy complexion, and so forth.

The imagination is the first to be accused by enlightened minds, and Michaël Ranft borrows the theories of the Italian doctor Scalinger (1484–1558) on this point.[14]

> We are however strongly compelled to admit that the powers of the imagination are vigorous enough to spur the development of the illness toward death. Scalinger deserves to be cited here for his contemplations of imaginary illnesses. "The malady of the imagination when phantoms invade the mind is called *phrénitis.* Another disease of the imagination is one the Greeks named *korubantiasmos.* Corybantism affects those who, sleeping with eyes open, cannot sleep peacefully, because of the images and noises sent them by the Corybants (priests of Cybele), if we believe the superstition of the Ancients."

His explanation of the vision of the dead by the living is resolutely modern. Attributed to "a very fervent imagination," it is based on:

. . . the sensation of images coming from the dead who, through their intervention, would have worked on them so strongly that they eventually died from frenetic delirium or another illness of the same nature. The survivors fearing to suffer the same fate, have turned the words of the dying people over and over in their mind and, when they think they heard them say, among other things, that the dead man had come to them and tormented them in all kinds of ways, they decided to exhume the cadaver and look for why he returned to torture the living by sending them such dreadful visions.[15]

Everything therefore is taking place in people's heads, and this observation relies primarily on the fact that it is first family members, then close friends who are attacked by vampires. What Ranft does not say, but which is obvious to us, is that the survivors had a reading grid based on precedents, and that everything that happened to them was reinterpreted through this grid.

Michaël Ranft combines the ideas of his time and offers the following conclusion:

However, we can deduce that the separation of the soul and its removal from the body specifically define the death of the man, which should be distinguished from the death of the body itself. . . . Man is composed, as we know, of two essential parts, the body and the soul. When one part dies, the man ceases to be a man, but the soul does not stop being a soul and the body does not cease to remain a body.[16]

He supports his argument on the writings of Theodore Craanen, who states "that it should not be thought that the human body dies because the soul has pulled out of the body; it is rather because the body pulls away from the mind that it dies . . . the organs necessary for a complete and controlled life are altered and corrupted to a point that the mind can no longer use them to send its commands through the body and fulfill its duties."[17] Ranft then concludes: "This is how, as long as the destructible body exists, it can also contain within itself a kind of life, if not with respect to the entire organism, at least with regard to homogenous parts among them."[18] In this way, the cadaver has a certain form of life, and this explains why the manifestations of vampires and other revenants do not cease until the body is utterly destroyed. The bloodsuckers and the chewers are kinds of soulless zombies, according to these theories, but the paradox persists, for they are able to attend to their wicked mischief, a sign that the brain or mind is transmitting orders to the limbs. In fact, the scientific theories explain everything that pertains to the "vegetative life of the corpse": the growth of the nails, the beard, and so forth.

Ranft did not rule out magic, and he refers to Johann Kozack: "Many people have been able to summon a natural, elementary spirit capable of sucking their milk and blood." Ranft's other explanations have a very modern character that may make them of interest to psychiatrists and other analysts. He mentions the bite of remorse, which corresponds to the current notion of the work of mourning, as well as fear. Let's take the example of Peter Plogojovitz, whom we cited earlier. Ranft gives the following explanation for him:

> This gallant man perished suddenly or violently. This death, whatever it is, can provoke in the survivors the visions they had after his death. Sudden death gives rise to inquietude in the familiar circle. Inquietude has sorrow as a companion. Sorrow brings melancholy. Melancholy engenders restless nights and tormenting dreams. These dreams enfeeble body and spirit until illness and eventually death overcome.[19]

What inspires the most food for thought is the absence of signs of decay in certain corpses, a scientifically verifiable fact, but one that is not pertinent. According to Garmann, "the worms have no right over the cadavers of those who lived forthrightly and honestly, and they will not crumble to dust until the hour that precedes the resurrection of the dead."[20] This can be due to the nature of the ground in which the dead have been interred, but also to the individual's birth date: "There are three days and three nights over the course of any year that are quite singular: January 27, January 30, and February 13; the bodies of those born on these dates will remain uncorrupted until the last day," states Baron von Valvassor. Johan Joachim Becher is more "scientific" when he notes that "the dry and hot individuals only decay with difficulty, better, there are some that never decay."

There is also the omnipresent notion of illness and epidemics in vampire stories. In 1663 the pastor Martin Böhm gave a sermon in which he brought up the events of 1553: "During the time of pestilence we have learned that the dead, especially the women carried off by the plague, chewed in their tombs, making the same noise as a sow eating; and the plague grew stronger simultaneously."[21] From the first narratives, which date from the end of the seventeenth century but traces of which can be found five centuries earlier, pestilences and other diseases are supposedly sent by the wicked dead—essentially, people who were feared or were suspect during their lifetimes. There is an implied tie with sorcery. People held the first to die responsible for all the deaths that followed, and the body of this victim was exhumed and burned. Eighteenth-century scholars concluded that the evil was actually spread by doing this—a very modern idea if ever there was one, although the idea of viruses and germs was unknown at this time. Johann Friedrich Weitenkampf gives us an excellent analysis of the evolution of the facts by borrowing the example of Arnod Paole. This man ate the poisoned earth from a vampire's grave and covered himself with its blood—and apparently, this was the origin of the epidemic. The emanations the grave released infected cattle when they passed near the grave, and people ate the meat of the cattle and children fed on the milk of their mothers who had eaten this food.[22]

It is the notion of the epidemic that, historically, encouraged the replacement of the persecution of witches with that of vampires. We can see this in the testimony of Inquisitors Henry Institoris and Jacques Sprenger, cited in chapter 4. One and all, they provoked deaths that were inexplicably saved by an evil spell. If these wizards or witches were dead, these are posthumous evil spells—the famous posthumous magic examined by Charles Ferdinand von Schertz in 1706. During an era when it was unknown how infectious diseases spread, people fell back on the old explanation that all the ills besetting a community were due to the malignant nature of certain individuals endowed with extraordinary powers or knowledge. The novelty here was that the evil spells could continue after the demise of these individuals.

Nikolaus Kyll has rightly emphasized how belief in the wicked dead surged during an epidemic, and he cites two recent Hungarian examples from the twentieth century: When an epidemic affected the village of Magyarlapád, the grave of a certain woman was opened after it was found that the body was not resting as it should be and was therefore causing the death of others. Her body was then turned over so that it was lying flat on its belly in the coffin with her face turned toward the ground. Around 1927, in the region of Previgye, the same steps were taken during a cholera epidemic.[23] Literature has recuperated this belief, and in 1861, in one of his vampire novels, Léon Gozlan notes: "Vampires . . . only ever appear in such great numbers during times of raging epidemics." We will recall that Murnau made use of this tradition in his *Nosferatu*.

I would now like to mention the most recent hypothesis to date, that of Wayne Tikkanen.[24] This chemistry professor at UCLA believes the vampire is an individual stricken with porphyria, a hereditary blood disease common in Transylvania. It causes the curled back lips, malformed teeth, hypertrichosis—an abnormally great growth of body hair—necrosis of the fingers and nose, darkening of the skin (which becomes overly sensitive to ultraviolet light), and the turning to toxin of one of the components of hemoglobin. Tikkanen explains that some of these sufferers hide in coffins to protect themselves from sunlight, and he comes to the same conclusions presented by L. Illis in his 1964 study of this affliction.[25]

Also contemporary is the theory of the Spanish neurologist Juan Gomez-Alonso, who has noted many similarities between vampires and individuals infected by rabies: they have periods of insomnia during which they wander; they are agitated and excessively sensitive to water, smells, and light; and some have contractions of the face, larynx, and pharynx, which causes them to make raucous noises and even creates a bloody foam around the corners of the mouth, because the saliva can no longer be swallowed. Spasms are triggered by water, light, or mirrors; when the rabid are in the crisis stage of the disease, they try to bite those around them; their sexual appetites are sometimes increased tenfold; and when they die, blood sometimes comes out of their mouths. There are certainly some amazing parallels between rabies victims and vampires, but to say that "the legends of vampires appear to have been born during a particularly lethal rabies epidemic in Hungary between 1721 and 1728, which especially affected dogs and wolves,"[26] is really jumping the gun and overlooks the fact that vampirism existed before this date. The most we can accept is that rabies may account for one of these epidemics, the more important ones being plague and cholera.* Whatever the case may be, Illis, Tikkanen, and Gomez-Alonzo testify, in their own way, to the fascination that the vampire myth continues to hold over even the most scientific minds desperately questing for an explanation. But none of the three seems to realize that they are dealing with a myth. They neglect all social, mental, and historical contexts and concentrate on one isolated motif—which causes some serious errors of method. Reading them might cause us to think that vampires were restricted to Transylvania, which, as we have seen, is not the case at all!

All that remains to be mentioned is the psychiatric explanation. According to this, vampires would be schizophrenics who had a dread of imprisonment and would go through cycles of exhaustion due to lack of food and a reversal of the diurnal and nocturnal cycles.[27] These are the conclusions presented by Lawrence Kayton in 1972.

The Denial of the Evidence

All enlightened minds, all those good rationalists and positivists, all those theologians who are confronted by something that conflicts with their

---

*Some descriptions of corpses or people on their deathbeds in *Le Hussard sur le toit* [a novel by French author Jean Giono the title of which translates as The Horseman on the Roof. —*Trans.*] are very suggestive in this regard. The novel shows, among other things, how the epidemic made people predisposed to acting irrationally or adopting irrational beliefs.

convictions founded on either long scientific study or Christian dogma—all offer explanations that are, in fact, exact reflections of their psyches, their ways of thinking. This is how they refuse to accept the popular belief that, for its part, evaluates the facts differently. When all our scholars and ecclesiastics advance terms such as *mind, soul, devil,* and *demon* to attempt to define what gives life to the cadaver, what animates the corpse, and what prevents its decay, they deny the evidence, draw nothing from their observations, and, most important, miss the essential point: the wicked dead and vampires cease their activity only when their bodies have been reduced to ashes. For some, the soul or spirit is then freed of the chains that shackled it and formed an obstacle to its departure for the next world, to passing over. For others, burning the body deprives the devil of his receptacle. These contemporary explanations or conclusions are merely beating around the bush and obscuring data of great antiquity.

In the remote past, an individual possessed several "souls," each attached to one of the parts of the body. There was the soul of the bones, the soul of the liver, that of the blood, and so on. During the Middle Ages, the lexicon of common languages attests to the survival of this belief, and the number of words designating the soul vary from three to five. Latin texts, meanwhile, attest to at least three terms: *animus, spiritus,* and *anima,* found especially in the clerical literature. The first designates the vital principle; the second is the mind or thought, which is to say the issuer of the orders to the animus; and the third is the immortal part of the human being, the one connecting the being to God. According to the Bible, humans are composed of three elements: the *nefash* (the persona), the *basar* (heart, kidney, liver—in other words, the body); and the *ruah* (the spirit communicated by God). The Greeks, meanwhile, knew the *thumos* (passion, will, mind); the *psuche* (life, breath)—according to Homer, the veritable tracing of the body—and it becomes the double (*eidolon*) of the individual at death, which shows itself in the form of a shadow (*skia*), smoke (*kapnos*), or a dream (*oneiros*).[28] Philology admirably vouches for this notion of the plural soul that was long retained in folk traditions. In our corpus, the belief comes through here and there, when the spirit is involved, as in the testimony of Hans Bürgel: while examining cadavers, this gravedigger declared that those who were spared putrefaction had a "strong spirit." This spirit or force was reinterpreted by the clerics as a devil, a convenient word that veils the reality of beliefs more than it elucidates them—and which encourages the interpretation into devil or demon.

Now we can sum up the facts. The activity of the dead was extinguished with the total destruction of their bodies. The individuals predestined to come back were essentially the marginal (at least early on), those reputed to have been born on a certain date or in certain circumstances, those who bore a particular mark, those who exercised a trade that put them in contact with the forces of nature or death—people, therefore, who are alleged to possess supernatural knowledge and gifts. It is only a step from them to wizards and seers. These characteristics became obvious after their deaths, which were necessarily abnormal. Among the revenants and vampires, a nonnegligible quantity were also made up of werewolves, especially in central Europe, and everywhere by those people who behaved as nightmares. It is due to all these special individuals that we are able to know what animates vampires.

Werewolves, wizards, seers, nightmares: all possessed the ability to double themselves—that is, to send forth their double (alter ego), the Ka of the ancient Egyptians, during sleep or when in a trance, and this double could just as easily take the form of an animal as a human.[29] Let's recall the transformations of Count Dracula: he can change into a wolf or a bat. In fact, this is not a metamorphosis, properly speaking: his body, like that of other revenants, is lying somewhere, and it is his double that shows itself in this way. This alter ego will survive as long as the body has not crumbled into dust. It is three-dimensional and has solid consistency; it is not an ethereal phantom or illusion but an exact copy of the body. We can recall the difficulty of all the authors in explaining how the vampire, or revenant, leaves his grave. For some, the sepulchre opens and closes itself upon its inhabitant; for others, it has an orifice that, however minuscule, permits passage. Edgar Morin was the first to distinguish this double in the beliefs connected to vampires: "Universally, decomposition is the terrible period when the body and the double are still mixed with each other, in which everything has not yet been accomplished, over which hovers a muted vampiric threat."[30] If we go back to the testimonies of the twelfth and thirteenth centuries, we find quite a different story: the revenant escaped by burrowing into the ground without leaving a trace, and when its grave was opened, irrefutable signs were found on it to tell that it was indeed the individual with whom the living had been grappling.[31] The belief in the double is perfectly sensible when the Romanians asserted that the strigoï possesses two souls, when the Slavs talked about *dvoeduschniki,* or when we learn the genesis of the stafia was the walled-up shadow of a living human being. It is equally visible in those folktales in which we are told that this or that character has hidden his soul somewhere and therefore cannot be slain until it is found.

Another detail of certain stories merits attention: Why must some vampires and revenants leave their shroud behind when they exit to attack the living? The shroud can be understood as the visible mark of the deceased's new status, and it can be added to another well-known belief: the loss of his shadow, which is one of his souls. The shroud represents the body that remains in the tomb after the double has left. The motif of the abandoned shroud appears as a reversal of the execution modalities of ordinary revenants that are slain by destroying their bodies—which is to say, by depriving their alter egos of support. Taking possession of the shroud that substitutes for the body prevents the double from reintegrating with it, therefore causing the death of the vampire.

To back up this hypothesis, we can look at a widespread theme in folk beliefs: when the alter ego or soul of a person has gone off on a journey and the body remains inanimate, it is especially important not to move it or turn it over. Doing so means the soul will not be able to enter it and the individual will die. This is what the documentation collected by Vera Meyer-Matheis shows us.[32] This also explains the wrath of the revenant who is unable to find his shroud, his efforts to take it back, and his relatively easy elimination, whether in the story of the haunting of the village of Egwanschitz, which Sheridan Le Fanu borrowed for *Carmilla,* or in the ballad by Goethe, in which the coming of dawn slays the emaciated corpse that scales the tower. Without his shroud, the revenant is unable to dive back into his grave, and he is made vulnerable, exposed to either the rays of the sun or to an instrument used by a living human being as a weapon.

This double, however, requires a motivation to act, and this is where we find the notions of vengeance, dissatisfaction, and malignancy that cause the wickedness of the de cujus and that spread terror throughout a region. Contrary to the revenants of the Middle Ages, vampires are no longer the guarantors of the social order and a system of moral values. Of course, good revenants exist, but their numbers are not legion and they essentially manifest in dreams. Much more numerous are those who have but one purpose in their posthumous life: to harm as many living as they can. Discontented with their lot for whatever reason, they wish to deprive the living of their happiness and prosperity, and therefore they attack their means of existence—livestock, for example—and even the very lives of their compatriots.

We should never forget that the vampire is only one form taken by revenants. He is a hematophile, an individual who, over the course of the centuries, has specialized in bloodsucking—what researchers have recognized as a form of cannibalism. We have seen earlier that revenants kill in a number of ways. In this sense the vampire is only one variety of this populace stuck between this world and the next, and this is where the modern myth was created. The major innovation of the modern myth was to subordinate the vampire's life to his blood diet, to instill the belief that he fed on what has long been regarded as the very essence of life. "Blood is life," exclaims the lunatic Renfield, a human vampire in Bram Stoker's novel, which brings to minds the words from Leviticus 17:11: "The life of the flesh is within the blood." To maintain his life through killing: such is the curse—if not the credo—of the vampire.

The literary fiction, however, has its flaws. The most serious of these, in the case of the very ancient dead, is their mode of survival in the grave, where they are deprived of the precious fluid. Everything takes place as if the dead is plunged into a kind of cataleptic stupor and has no more than a vegetative form of life, a latent state from which he will emerge, provided he ingest just a few drops of blood. This same notion is the basis for the scenario in *The X-Files* in which a living being needs only to pass within close proximity of an extraterrestrial monster in order for the alien to invade him and allow it to come back to life. This notion is particularly visible in Théophile Gautier's book, during Clarimonde's sudden decline.

> For some time the health of Clarimonde had not been so good as usual; her complexion grew paler day by day. The physicians who were summoned could not comprehend the nature of her malady and knew not how to treat it. They all prescribed some insignificant remedies, and never called a second time. Her paleness, nevertheless, visibly increased, and she became colder and colder, until she seemed almost as white and dead as upon that memorable night in the unknown castle.

What Gautier implies is that the vampire will die if deprived too long of the vital fluid. The difference between Clarimonde and Count Dracula is obvious. Among the earlier authors, artistic vagueness is the rule: Polidori does not raise the matter and even shows Lord Ruthven slain by the blow from a dagger, then coming back to life elsewhere when exposed to moonlight.

It is these ambiguities that create the fantasy atmosphere of the later Gothic novels. They forged the myth while allowing uncertainty to remain: mortal or immortal? No one truly knows! Victim or executioner? Who is truly capable of answering this question? Some filmmakers have seen clearly that what they are working with is a kind of philosophical tale, a long meditation on the notions of life and death, and in the role of Dracula, German actor Klaus Kinski lets it be known that immortality is a heavy burden.

But what does the myth tell us? If we look at the etymological definition of the term *myth,* it is a language, thus the carrier of a message with a universal value, the fruit of a vision of the world and an explanation of questions inspired by life. It tells us of the inaccuracies of the stories of Christianity, the dominant religion, it tells us that there are no clearly marked boundaries between the states of life and death: the dead person still has an existence and can speak and move, provided he has been given a reason. This existence emerges clearly from the trials that can be instituted against the dead, their condemnations, and their executions. They are still a persona in the legal sense of the word, both responsible for their actions and for answering to them before society. The myth calls back into question the body/soul duality and continues to transport the notion of the plural soul: each part of the body has its own. This would explain the survival of the vampire as well as his desperate search for fresh blood: the vampire is one way of appropriating a soul, therefore life.

Plunging its roots into the heart of ancient beliefs, the myth therefore offers us both an exposé of the problems and their solution: the dead are dangerous. Treat them well, otherwise you will have every reason to dread them. This myth borrows the notions of the good and bad death, of passing away as reward for an honest and just life, and the notion of a posthumous punishment. This monster does not sleep in the ground and he does not rest in peace: this is his punishment. He is an exile and outlaw who, according to the stories, can still find redemption with the help of the living. Slaying vampires is therefore a pious action, it frees them from the last shackles that prevent them from soaring into the stars, toward that otherworld over which mystery still hangs. Bram Stoker expresses it perfectly:

> There, in the coffin lay no longer the foul Thing that we had so dreaded and grown to hate that the work of her destruction was yielded as a privilege to the one best entitled to it, but Lucy as we had seen her in life, with her face of unequalled sweetness and purity.... One and all we felt that the holy calm that lay like sunshine over the wasted face and form was only an earthly token and symbol of the calm that was to reign forever.

In the end, the modern myth of the vampire leads to a contemplation of life, death, and love, the three essential roots of our humanity. Is not life a dream and death a slumber from which we will emerge one day thanks to the power of love or hate, those two great forces that presided over Creation, according to the ancient Chaldean mythologies?

The Vampires of Medvegia

IT IS COMMON KNOWLEDGE that myth creates its own proof, and that in past eras, myths were essentially the narratives of trustworthy eyewitnesses. Yet often the actors in the drama have an entirely subjective view of the facts, which they interpret in accordance with their assumptions. An excellent example of this can be found in the narrative supplied by Pitton de Tournefort of the exhumation of a broucolaca on the island of Mykonos.[1] We can first consider the report of some individuals who were not predisposed to see beyond reality.

In 1732 the Austrian authorities opened an investigation into about fifteen suspicious deaths that had occurred in the locale of Medvegia in Turkish Serbia.[2] The witnesses were deposed, then the graves were opened. On some of the cadavers there was incontestable evidence proving they were vampires: their bodies were filled with blood and had not decayed. The report is of great historical interest because it gives us an opening into the mind-set of that time and reveals how phenomena that can be explained by contemporary science played a preponderant role in the belief in vampires. This report was the origin for a flood of treatises on vampires, and it was often reprinted—and even sharply criticized, notably by the Prussian Academy of Sciences.[3]

> After it had been reported that in the village of Medvegia the so-called vampires had killed some people by sucking their blood, I was, by high decree of a local Honourable Supreme Command, sent there

to investigate the matter thoroughly, along with officers detailed for that purpose and two subordinate medical officers, and therefore carried out and heard the present inquiry in the company of the captain of the Stallath Company of haiducs, Hadnack Gorschiz, the bariactar and the oldest haiduc of the village, as follows: who unanimously recount that about five years ago a local haiduc by the name of Arnod Paole broke his neck in a fall from a hay wagon. This man had, during his lifetime, often revealed that, near Gossowa in Turkish Serbia, he had been troubled by a vampire, wherefore he had eaten from the earth of the vampire's grave and smeared himself with the vampire's blood in order to be free of the vexation he had suffered. In twenty or thirty days after his death some people complained that they were being bothered by this same Arnod Paole; and in fact four people were killed by him. In order to end this evil, they dug up this Arnod Paole forty days after his death—this on the advice of their hadnack, who had been present at such events before; and they found that he was quite complete and undecayed, and that fresh blood had flowed from his eyes, nose, mouth, and ears; that the shirt, the covering, and the coffin were completely bloody; that the old nails on his hands and feet, along with the skin had completely fallen off, and that new ones had grown; and since they saw from this that he was a true vampire, they drove a stake through his heart, according to their custom. Whereby he gave an audible groan and bled copiously. Thereupon they burned the body on the same day to ashes and threw these into the grave. These same people say further that all those who were tormented and killed by the vampires must themselves become vampires. Thereupon they disinterred the above-mentioned four people in the same way. Then they also add that this Arnod Paole attacked not only the people but also the cattle, and sucked out their blood. And since the people used the flesh of such cattle, it appears that some vampires are again present here, inasmuch as, in a period of three months, seventeen young and old people died, among them some who, with no previous illness, died in two or at the most three days. In addition, the haiduc Jowiza reports that his stepdaughter, by the name of Stanacka, lay down to sleep fifteen days ago, fresh and healthy, but at midnight she started up out of her sleep with a terrible cry, fearful and trembling, and complained that she had been throttled by the son of a haiduc by the name of Milloe, who had died nine weeks earlier, whereupon she had experienced a great pain in the chest and became worse hour by hour, until finally she died on the third day. At this we went the same afternoon to the graveyard, along with the often-mentioned oldest haiducs of the village, in order to cause the suspicious graves to be opened and to examine the bodies in them, whereby, after all of them had been dissected, there was found:

1. A woman by the name of Stana, twenty years old, who had died in childbirth two months ago, after a three-day illness, and who had herself said, before her death, that she had painted herself with the blood of a vampire, wherefore both she and her child—which had died right after birth and because of a careless burial had been half eaten by dogs—must also become vampires. She was quite complete and undecayed. After the opening of the body there was found in the cavitate pectoris a quantity of fresh extravascular blood. The vasa of the arteriae and venae, like the ventriculis cordis were not, as is usual, filled will coagulated blood, and the whole viscera, that is the pulmo, hepar, stomachus, lien, and intestina, were quite fresh as they would be in a healthy person. The uterus was however quite enlarged in place, wherefore the same was in complete putredine. The skin on her hands and feet, along with the old nails, fell away on their own, but on the other hand completely new nails were evident, along with a fresh and vivid skin.

2. There was a woman by the name of Miliza (sixty years old, incidentally), who had died after a three-month sickness and had been buried ninety-some days earlier. In the chest, much liquid blood was found, and the other viscera were, like those mentioned

before, in a good condition. During her dissection, all the haiducs who were standing around marveled greatly at her plumpness and perfect body, uniformly stating that they had known the woman well, from her youth, and she had, throughout her life, looked and been very lean and dried up, and they emphasized that she had come to this startling plumpness in the grave. They also said that it was she who had started the vampires this time, because she had eaten the flesh of those sheep that had been killed by the previous vampires.

3. There was an eight-day-old child who had lain in the grave for ninety days and was similarly in a condition of vampirism.

4. The son of a haiduc, sixteen years old, was dug up, having lain in the earth for nine weeks, after he had died from a three-day illness, and was found like the other vampires.

5. Joachim, also the son of a haiduc, seventeen years old, had died after a three-day illness. He had been buried eight weeks and four days and, on being dissected, was found in a similar condition.

6. A woman by the name of Ruscha who had died after a ten-day illness and had been buried six weeks previous, in whom there was much fresh blood not only in the chest but also in fundo ventriculi. The same showed itself in her child, which was eighteen days old and had died five weeks previously.

7. No less did a girl of ten years of age, who had died two months previously, find herself in the above-mentioned condition, quite complete and undecayed, and had much fresh blood in her chest.

8. They caused the wife of the hadnack to be dug up, along with her child. She had died seven weeks previously, her child—who was eight weeks old—had died twenty-one days previously, and it was found that both mother and child were completely decomposed, although earth and graves were like those of the vampires lying nearby.

9. A servant of the local corporal of the haiducs, by the name of Rhade, twenty-three years old, died after a three-month-long illness, and

after a five-week burial was found completely decomposed.

10. The wife of the local bariactar, along with her child, having died six weeks previously, I noticed a profuse liquid blood, like the others, in the chest and stomach. The entire body was in the oft-named condition of vampirism.

11. With Stanche, a haiduc, sixty years old, who had died six weeks previously, I noticed a profuse liquid blood, like the others, in the chest and stomach. The entire body was in the oft-named condition of vampirism.

12. Milloe, a haiduc, twenty-five years old, who had lain for six weeks in the earth was also found in the condition of vampirism mentioned.

13. Stanoicka, the wife of a haiduc, twenty years old, died after a three-day illness and had been buried eighteen days previously. In the dissection I found that she was in her countenance quite red and of a vivid color, and as mentioned above, she had been throttled at midnight, by Milloe, the son of the haiduc, and there was also to be seen, on the right side under the ear, a bloodshot blue mark the length of a finger. As she was being taken out of the grave, a quantity of fresh blood flowed from her nose. With the dissection I found, as mentioned often already, a regular fragrant fresh bleeding, not only in the chest cavity but also in venriculo cordis. All the viscera found themselves in a completely good and healthy condition. The hypodermis of the entire body, along with the fresh nails on hands and feet, was as though completely fresh. After the examination had taken place, the heads of the vampires were cut off by the local gypsies and then burned along with the bodies, and then the ashes were thrown into the river Morava. The decomposed bodies, however, were laid back into their own graves. Which I attest along with those assistant medical officers provided for me. Actum ut spra:

(L.S.) Johannes Fluchinger, Regiment Medical officer of the Foot Regiment of the Honourable B. Fursstenbusch

(L.S.) J. H. Sigel, Medical officer of the Honourable Morall Regiment

(L.S.) Johann Friedrich Baumgarten, Medical officer of the
Foot Regiment of the Honourable B. Furstenbusch

The undersigned attest herewith that all that which the Regement
Medical officer of the Hourable Furstenbusch Regiment had
observed in the matter of vampires—along with both of the medical
officers who have signed with him—is in every way truthful and has
been undertaken, observed, and examined in our own presence. In
confirmation thereof is our signature in our own hand, of our own
making.

BELGRADE, JANUARY 26, 1732

Büttener,
FIRST LIEUTENANT OF
THE HONOURABLE ALEXANDER
REGIMENT OF WURTEMBERG

J. H. von Lindenfels,
STANDARD-BEARER OF
THE HONOURABLE ALEXANDER
REGIMENT OF WURTEMBERG

The Dead Woman's Shroud

GOETHE AS WELL AS Sheridan Le Fanu found inspiration in an ancient legend whose tone was set by Selt in 1833: after leading a dissolute life, a woman returned to the city of Wroclaw.[1] This little news item should be compared to the ballad "The Bride of Corinth" by Goethe, cited in the introduction.

> What had already been assumed and said about her when still alive turned out to be true: the wicked woman knew no rest in her grave. The watchman of St. Elizabeth Tower noted with terror that every night, when the hour of the spirits sounded, this person would emerge from her sepulchre, cast her shroud on the mound, and leave briskly for her home, where, for an entire hour, she would ceaselessly measure out remnants of cloth, measuring endlessly until the sweat beaded up on her forehead and her eyes bled.*
>
> One night, having ascertained that the revenant had left her tomb, cast down her shroud, and was busy elsewhere about her affairs, the watchman descended from the tower, made his way to the grave, grabbed the shroud, and returned to his post. When he went to

---

*Damnation takes the form of the eternal repetition of an action. This is reminiscent of Sisyphus.

close the little door and begin climbing the circular staircase, an idea suddenly occurred to him, and he prudently drew the sign of the cross three times on the door. He then closed it and started climbing rapidly, the old shroud over his arm, and then he tossed the shroud on a small wooden altar. He went to the window from where, in one glance, he could see the entire cemetery and the graves.

It was forty-five minutes past midnight, and the revenant had returned to her dwelling. Not finding her shroud, her gaze turned immediately toward the little window where the watchman was indiscreetly watching the scene before starting back with fright on seeing her furious gestures. His fear grew even greater, however, when he saw that the revenant was briskly making her way to the tower. The closer she approached, the more terrified he became. He clasped his hands in prayer and his lips stammered without his knowing. The dead woman was now at the doorway. She saw the sign of the cross and recoiled with a shudder. The horrified watchman was leaning a little farther out the window. When he saw the effect produced by the cross, he started to head for his lodging to give thanks to God, but when he cast a final glance back to see if the revenant had retreated, he saw to his horror that she had started scaling the outside of the tower.* Panic seized him, and his limbs froze as if petrified. He could no longer leave the window, and he remained there, fascinated, watching the other getting closer and closer. He could already make out her face convulsed with rage and bathed by the moon in a pale light. His hair stood up on his head. The revenant arrived at the sill and pulled herself up as the watchman collapsed to the floor with a cry of terror. The hour of one sounded. Immediately, the bones of the emaciated hands lost their grip on the balustrade and the legs no longer gripped the pillar around which they were enlaced, and with a great tumult, the dead woman fell to the hard ground of the cemetery.

The next day, the terribly damaged but still recognizable body of this cursed woman was found. The people, who in the meantime

---

*This brings to mind Count Dracula scaling down the facade of his castle like a lizard.

had heard about this horrible incident—after which the watchman had fallen ill from the terror he had experienced—would not tolerate the body being buried again in consecrated ground. The hangman was summoned: he cut off the head with a spade and, placing the body on a cowhide, interred it beneath the gibbet. The watchman did not long survive that terrible night,* but the revenant was never seen again. This terrifying event was carved in metal by an artist, and the image could be seen until the beginning of this century on one of the portals of Saint Elizabeth Church, hidden on the side of one of the walls.†

---

*In 95 percent of the cases, the encounter with a revenant is fatal.
†Proof and justification of the event's reality.

APPENDIX 3

The Vampire
of Bendschin
or Pentsch

IN 1592 THE MARKET TOWN of Bendschin, or Pentsch, home of the principality of Jägerndorf on the Moravian frontier, became famous because of a series of events that occurred there, for which we have a narrative that is ethnographical. It is a veritable piece of reporting on the misdeeds of a vampire[1] whose author is Martin Weinreich (1548–1609), a professor in Breslau. What merits our attention is that it permits us to follow, step by step, the emergence of beliefs that explained the transformation of a dead man into a vampire. The principal stages are easily defined, and the mechanism structuring the thought of contemporaries regarding this event is particularly clear.

1. A man dies unexpectedly—from the kick if a horse—and therefore suspiciously, which inspires contemplation and interrogation. People begin to chatter about it.
2. Everyone recalls everything that might explain this sudden death, and the most innocent incidents become signs of another, hidden reality—one that is dark and smells of brimstone. The deceased is lying in the church: there is the burst of a storm during the

interment and the gesture made by the cadaver when it is laid out. This suggests that he may have had knowledge of his imminent demise. Everything is therefore reinterpreted by means of an archetypal thought.

3. People fall back to the simplest explanation: the dead man had undoubtedly concluded a pact with the devil. He was a wizard, and the demon had possessed the murderous horse to make his death acceptable to the community so that there would be no obstacle to the funeral rituals.

4. The return of the dead man and his criminal acts confirm the correctness of the interpretation, but other explanations are suggested: The deceased was concerned about the fate of his youngest son and feared that he would be despoiled, which proves he did not leave with his affairs in order. He comes to seek revenge on the horse that killed him.

5. People hesitate over the true nature of the revenant—spirit or devil?—who behaves like a poltergeist, a nightmare, and a vampire, attacking man and beast, and who plays a number of mean tricks, which makes him akin to mischievous goblins or sprites.

6. The tomb is opened and there is found confirmation of everyone's wildest suspicions.

7. The corpse is legally executed.

The text is chock-full of revelatory details, even if not all of them are explained, which is usual, for they formed part of what our ancestors considered common knowledge and regarded as self-evident. I provide subheads here to permit you to better understand the text, and I have italicized those details that are most meaningful.

Johann Cuntze (Johannes Cuntius), First Rumors

A citizen of this town, Johann Cuntze, born in the village of Lichten, conducted himself as was proper for many years deserving all possible praise, even being named to the (municipal) council and then elected mayor. He was regarded as an experienced sexagenarian of high worth, and his advice was sought for all manner of municipal and personal matters. It was only after his death that sins were attributed to him that had been hushed up during his lifetime. In fact, the parson of the parish began by saying that he had frequented the church assiduously, had attended communion with reverence, but that *he had also frequently slept* in his counselor's chair. It was not by chance that Cuntze had been named a judge with other council members, because of certain quarrels between a Hungarian merchant and his waggoners. He led an investigation and made his report to the court. The two parties were heard, a protocol was drawn up, then Mrs. Cuntze invited all to supper, but on the pretext of domestic duties to attend to, her husband did not wish to linger and said that it is best to make merry while one is able for there are no shortage of daily vicissitudes. He owned five splendid horses in his stable and when he returned, ordered the best of them brought out and tied to a column near the door so that a horseshoe that was threatening to fall off could be reattached. While he was doing this with the help of a stablehand, he lifted the horse's hoof, but the animal was suddenly filled with rage and kicked out, hurling master and servant half dead to the ground. A neighbor witnessing the scene rushed in and helped them to get back up, then brought them back into the house. Cuntze began yelling immediately, complaining about atrocious pain and burning, and did not stop until his bed had been prepared and he was laid down upon it and his chest, where he felt this terrible burning, was exposed. *One saw no trace of any wound* although he continued moaning. In the meantime his youngest son of a third union had come close to his bed. Cuntze looked at him with pity and told him: "Alas, poor child, I would have liked to live yet a few more years for you!" He warmly recommended him to one of his fellow council members who was also his godfather, and the man promised to look out for him. His son consoled the ailing man by telling him it was in God's power to raise him from his bed of misery. Cuntze responded: "Alas! If only God wished to forgive me my sins out of love for my son!" Those present did their best to comfort him and advised him to summon a priest, but he would have none of it and tirelessly repeated these words: "Alas! If only God would grant me His grace!" Touching his body, those there found his body and hands were as cold as ice although he was constantly complaining of the torrid heat. The horse had struck him on February 4 and someone had said that Cuntze had been a godfather again four days earlier, on the day of the Purification of the Virgin, and on returning while getting out of his clothes had said to other family members: *This will undoubtedly be the last child I hold over the baptismal fonts.* His wife and children therefore suspected he knew the hour of his death and had therefore had ties with the devil. In fact he had amassed quite a fortune* although he had not inherited anything, and had worked hard to earn a living first as a logger† and then manufacturing shingles. After his death, some said that he had been bonded with Satan while still alive so that the latter *killed him with the kick of a horse* so folk would not cause a scandal. In the meantime his eldest son, who lived not far away, had been alerted about the accident. He came and watched over his father the entire night.

Death and Interment

As the bells struck three o'clock, Cuntze died. Earlier, a large *black cat* had managed to open the casement window with his paw and suddenly bounded into the chamber, leaping onto the bed and attacking the pillow and the dying man's face with such violence that one would have said it was trying to forcefully remove him. It then vanished, and Cuntze breathed his last.

The next morning, Cuntze's eldest son went to visit the pastor

---

*During this time, the acquisition of sudden wealth was attributed to the possession of a familiar spirit called a *drac,* a silver or mandrake mannequin.
†A suspect profession.

with a high number of relatives. He announced the death of his father to him and asked for a funeral service worthy of his rank, as he had been a council member. This was granted him and he was entombed in the church to the right of the altar, but they paid a good price for this privilege.

Cuntze had barely died and a *terrible storm* burst out and, when his body was being carried to its final resting place, it snowed and thundered so violently that his pallbearers could barely stand it, but this all came to a halt once the dead man was interred. The weather brightened and the wild winds subsided. We should not forget to mention here that the moment when two poor women had tried to wash the body in a small tub and tried to place his hands behind his back, *the cadaver had violently put one hand back where he had been kicked.* One of the women was distressed but the other told her: "Keep quiet so that our gossiping does not cause any misfortune."*

The First Hauntings

Several days after the interment, a rumor spread through town that a *nightmare* or a *diabolical spirit* wearing the likeness of Cuntze had appeared and it had attacked a woman in the neighborhood, throwing her to the ground and molesting her, and this had happened on the very eve of his burial. After the interment, this same spirit had entered the room of one who was sleeping, woke him up, and shouted: "I am having the greatest difficulty restraining myself from beating you to death!" This was reported to the widow Cuntze, and the men of the watch admitted that every night a *horrible noise* was to be heard from the dead man's house,[2] objects were tossed about and dropped there, and in the morning the doors that had been tightly locked the night before were open and the horses were so

---

*This was a common mind-set during the Middle Ages. It is usually cited in the case of dreams: people refused to reveal their dreams' content for fear these dreams would come true.

agitated in the stables that one would have said they were being tormented or else biting and striking one another. A maidservant told one honorable man that she had awoken in fear early in the morning because she heard someone riding around the house and *banging into the walls* with such violence that the beams shook, and that a *clear light* was *coming in through the window*. This caused her to hide under the bed in terror. When she rose the man had left; she examined all the walls and saw in the freshly fallen snow strange tracks that were neither of a man nor an animal.*

February 24, after catechism, the parson of the village visited one of the local judges who was indisposed and who sharply addressed the cleric this way: "Ah, my dear colleague, last night I saw Cuntze at my home and I spoke with him." As the parson expressed his astonishment about such an impossible thing, the other replied haughtily: "I saw him last night at eleven o'clock with my own eyes and I heard him tell me: 'Fear nothing, dear colleague, I shall not harm you; I come only to discuss something with you. I have left my last-born Jacob, your godson; Stephen, my eldest son has a chest at his home that contains 450 florins; I want to reveal this to you so that *Jacob will not be slighted* of these florins. I charge you with faithfully looking after his interests. If you do not do this, you shall see what happens to you!'"† This man was the clerk of the municipal court, and he promised the ghost his honest service. The other vanished from the room but made such a racket on the next floor that everything shook, then he made his way to the stable where he tormented the cattle in the most atrocious way—one would have said that it sounded like they had gotten loose—but the next day everything was found as it should be.

The court clerk's house stood near that of Cuntze where, every night, the spirit caused such a heartrending commotion that the entire family sought refuge in the common room and hired watch-

---

*This imprecision is the sign of the intervention of supernatural forces.

†The absence of arrangements in his will for his son is therefore one of the causes of his return.

men to take turns guarding them. There were several bold young blades among them who had offered their services because they had been drinking. Then, when the spirit opened and closed doors, went into the kitchen and cellar, as well as into the common room where everyone had gathered, casting a glance into the room from the doorway and looking like Cuntze, they shouted at him: "Come in and stay, you trickster! What a cautious host you make in the night you who did not manage your property this way in the middle of the day and were stingy! Why are you so zealous when in the shadows, old scoundrel? Come in and have a drink with us!" In a room above the common room there were old and new iron objects and chains that the spirit cast about pell-mell in horrible fashion.* He tormented the horses so badly that one would have said he meant to strangle them,† especially the one that had struck him so violently in front of the door, he left that one no rest night and day, and while the others lay down being quickly exhausted, this one remained standing, sweating and trembling until it seemed it was destined to end up at the slaughterhouse. It was thus believed that the devil was in this beast that had killed Cuntze by kicking him with its shoe. Its sweat was always icy cold as Cuntze's had been, and as the animal had caused his master's demise, many wondered if it, too, should not be tossed into the pyre with Cuntze's corpse as a diabolical instrument to be burned.

By the wan light of candles and even lanterns, the family deliberated on the invisible presence of the devilish spirit, waking each other up. Because, when they slept, something crushed and exhausted them so that they needed to be revived with water and rescued from death like unconscious folk. Numerous times, even the sleepers were afflicted in the most horrible way despite the presence of the watchers by their side,‡ so horribly smothered that they vio-

---

*The theme of the poltergeist.
†An action generally attributed to a domestic spirit who is unhappy about the color of the animals placed under its guardianship.
‡Cuntze therefore behaves like a nightmare.

lently thrashed their feet, and even costly medicines had difficulty bringing them back. The widow had a maidservant sleep in her bed with her, but the spirit ordered her to leave if she did not want her neck broken. The widow then went to stretch out in the common room with her people who endured a thousand torments from the spirit who often appeared in his shroud, seated behind the stove. The widow had the worst lot because she could not enter another room without risk: the spirit was visible everywhere and even tried to make her lie with him. He drank the milk from the crocks and played a thousand tricks. He shouted at the youngest child: "Follow me into the grave and I shall give you many sous!"* His eldest son returned from the country to live in the paternal house, but the revenant made such a hubbub in his chamber that he could not fall asleep there for a long time despite his prayers and devotions. One family member could not repress his curiosity to see what the phantom did at night. He went into the hallway, encountered Cuntze, jumped back into the common room in a single leap, and collapsed to the ground. The other had crushed and tried to strangle him so tightly that he lost his strength and the marks he left remained quite visible on his throat and body the next day, which quenched any remaining enthusiasm he might have for acting imprudently. In the morning the spirit personally showed itself to many but at night it was unleashed, as if he wished to knock down entire houses. He tore from the ground and flung aside a large column that two men would have had trouble carrying.† Outside town he was recognized by many folk riding about on *a horse with three hooves* and the same color as his favorite mount. . . . He rode like a madman through town and field, and fire sprung out beneath him from his sides.‡

A lazy maidservant had gone to sleep before her mistress had returned; as at her return the food remained to be prepared and the

---

*Here, Cuntze possesses the nature of a summoner.
†Introduction of the theme of the supernatural strength of revenants.
‡He is therefore riding a diabolical horse with an odd number of feet, a sign of its belonging to the otherworld.

dishes to be washed, the spirit loomed up, opened the doors of the house, the common room, and the bedchambers, approached the woman's bed, touched her arm with his icy hand, and asked her why she left the dishes dirty on Thursday night.* The common folk of Jägernsdorf have an old superstition that says one should avoid doing household chores and the dishes during the twelve nights that separate Christmas from the New Year, as well as on Mondays, Thursdays, and Sundays. . . .

Following is a list of his other crimes: he crushed the legs of a child, trampled two old men to death, pressed the breast of a woman in labor, snatched children out of their cradles, almost suffocated an old woman, tried to rape women, demanded the settlement of a debt, tricked a drunkard.

Signs and Intersigns

A folly of the common folk says that where wizards or *Bilweise*† are buried, *holes are clearly visible in the mason work of their tombs,* as if mice had come out. A hole of this nature was found in Cuntze's tomb; it was even quite large and deep, so deep that one could touch the coffin with a staff. The slab was taken off, the hole and the grave were filled with dirt, and all was firmly packed down. The next day, the hole was gaping wide again and even larger than before, as if chickens had been scratching beneath the stone. Large spots of blood appeared on the altar cloth, and many nobles saw them . . .

A New Series of Exactions

Cuntze bit and beat a man, threw clumps of dirt on women lying near their husbands, appeared with eyes of fire, transformed into a pole, danced in the fields, hurled dogs against walls, sucked cows

---

*Here, Cuntze takes up the ancient role of fairies and household spirits who supervise the good order of the *domus.*

†Another local name for wizards.

and knotted their tails together, devoured chicks, bound the feet of goats and tossed them into the troughs, sucked and slew calves, mistreated horses, gave a sound buffet to a skeptic, squeezed the parson and his family with all his might, and grunted like a sow.*

On the evening of July 8, the parson was sitting near his wife and children, playing the organ, when an *intolerable stench* spread suddenly through the room and sent everyone fleeing. When the parson went to his room after a fervent evening prayer, the smell made its presence felt there in a quarter hour in all its horror, and the good parson heard the revenant approaching his bed, breathing upon him a vapor so cold and pestilential that he fell ill, with his face swelling and his eyes occasioned much suffering.

For all these reasons the town of Bendschin lost its reputation: no noble wished to set foot there anymore, no traveler would spend the night, and the inhabitants no longer knew which saint to give their devotions.

Exhumation and Execution

They thought to open several tombs to examine the cadavers because, for many years in similar circumstances, this measure had proved beneficial. His worship, the parson, brought up arguments of theology and physiology in opposition, the aggrieved inhabitants paid no attention and were all in accord to spare not the tomb of any family and to keep searching until they had found the source of their woes, have it blocked up, and its resident turned aside. They asked the parson for the keys [of the church], and after much debate, the sacristan handed them over. At their command, the gravedigger opened several tombs, including those of people who had died before Cuntze and after him, to examine the corpses and form an opinion. They claimed *there existed certain signs on the limbs of the departed* by which it could be recognized if they had been good Christians or

---

*This final detail is reminiscent of the chewers whose mastication is always accompanied by porcine grunts.

if they had concluded a *pact with Satan* and had died in a state of mortal sin.

Once they had opened the tomb and coffin of Cuntze and the others, they found that his cadaver exhibited a notorious difference; all the others who had died before or after him were already greatly putrefied or in a state of decay whereas he was *intact, fresh, and whole;* only the skin of his chest and head were black because quicklime had been placed in the coffin with the corpse so that it would quickly decompose. Beneath the surface layer of skin, which could easily be rubbed away, another skin was found that was firmer, fresh, and ruddy in color; all *his joints were supple* and his limbs mobile. A test was performed: a staff was placed in the cadaver's right hand and he gripped it firmly with his fingers. *His eyes were sometimes open, sometimes closed,* and when the corpse was lifted up, *he turned his head,* first toward midnight, then the next day at noon. Someone dared remove one of his stockings; underneath everything was intact: *the skin was reddish* with the arteries clearly visible. When his other calf was opened with a knife, *deep-red blood* flowed out as if from a living man. The nose, which rots first on the dead was intact and prominent. During his lifetime, Cuntze had been small and lean, but his cadaver had become much stronger, and his face and cheeks were swollen, and everything else had expanded like in pigs who are being raised and fattened, so much so that there was hardly any room left in the coffin in which he had been lying from February 8 to July 20.

To avoid rushing matters, council was held with men from the neighboring area learned in such affairs, but no one was found through them that did not blame Cuntze for everything that had happened. He was therefore condemned to be burned, but execution of the sentence was not carried out before explaining the entire affair to the court of the prince regent and receiving instructions on how to proceed. The first response said: do not rush; take other counsel and get more information, but inasmuch as the inhabitants have had enough of this diurnal and nocturnal disorder, make an agreement with a hangman from a neighboring town—they did not have one there at that time—for him to come with two assistants to carry out the cremation.

The inhabitants promised the hangman Cuntze's horse, a little money, and room and board for as long as he remained among them to carry out this matter. In the meantime, all the necessary preparations were made and men were ordered to dig a hole in the wall near the altar through which the carcass could be removed. All the inhabitants without exception made their way to a felling area belonging to the late Cuntze in a nearby wood, cut down what was needed, and brought it to the execution site where they erected a bonfire pile with the help of the hangman's assistants.

The body was pulled out of the tomb with ropes[3] and passed through *the hole in the wall.** The body proved so heavy that the ropes broke and people feared it would be impossible to move it. Outside the refuse cart to which Cuntze's horse had been attached was waiting. Carrying the cadaver was so difficult that this robust animal often had to stop and could only be urged to move forward by being struck, yet it had pulled the cart there effortlessly before, with both assistants sitting within it, both of whom were quite sturdy fellows. When they reached the waste dump,[†] they placed the body on the pyre with its shroud and *a clump of dirt placed at its throat,* and then lit the fire.

Although the flames were blazing and the body had been placed within them for quite a while, all that had been burned were the head, the forearms, and the lower part of the legs below the knees: the torso remained almost intact. The hangman pulled it out of the fire with a pitchfork and cut it into pieces, which were so filled with blood he was splattered all over by it. The fairly fatty flesh was tossed back into the fire one piece at a time, but it consumed the body so slowly because of all the blood contained by the corpse that the

*People avoided touching the corpse. Isidore of Seville informs us: "Impure is he . . . who has touched a dead man."

†So as not to soil the earth, an impure location was chosen.

cremation went on until late in the evening.* A fire was also made upon the ground where the body had been dismembered because quite a bit of blood had spread there. Guards were posted there for the night, and the next morning *the remaining ashes were tossed into the river with the earth from the tomb,* which was then filled with stones so that no one else could ever be interred there.

It was also whispered that the parents and brothers of Cuntze's second wife should be exhumed and burned because of hauntings that had followed their deaths—the ghosts had adopted their likenesses—on the order of the authorities of their jurisdiction, as they may also have led Cuntze to conclude a similar *pact with the devil.*

A New Haunting

The Satanic agitation ceased immediately following the execution. When asked, the night watchmen answered that nothing had happened. When crossing one another's paths, the inhabitants congratulated each other for the general tranquillity, as if the bright sunshine and cloudless sky had calmed down after a violent storm and heavy downpour. Things remained this way for a while, until a maidservant from Cuntze's house died and was buried.

Because she was suspected of having possibly learned something from the late Cuntze and been infected by the poison of sorcery, efforts were made to prevent her disturbing return by placing various items in her coffin: a nail from a wheel, a silver sou, the straw broom with which she habitually swept the kitchen,† and *a clump of fresh turf that was placed at her throat in between her chin and her chest.* All of this was intended to prevent any kind of evil spell, but all these measures were in vain.

---

*These details are perfectly real and are corroborated by modern stories of creamation. All cadavers do not burn alike.

†Everyone knows that the broom is the witch's chief instrument. The allusion to washing refers to the weather-working activity of these women, who cause storms by stirring their brooms in water. The nail and the sou are metallic objects that are meant to repel any spirits that desire to take possession of the cadaver.

Eight days after her death, a rapping spirit appeared and *squeezed* the other servants so tightly that their eyes swelled. It snatched an infant from its cradle and would have *strangled* it if the wet nurse had not raced in and rescued it while shouting the name of Jesus repeatedly. The next night it entered the stable in the shape of a chicken. Another maidservant believed it was a bird that had escaped from the henhouse so she tried to catch it, but the bird grew so enormously in size in an instant then grabbed her by the throat and pinched her so hard she bloated. After experiencing the terror this caused her, the maidservant was unable to eat or drink for several days and took Communion to prepare for a death she thought imminent. The spirit ordered a third maidservant to put on a white shirt because the one she was wearing was so dirty it needed to be washed.* The unrest lasted for an entire month, taking many forms. The revenant made atrociously loud raps on doors, squeezed and pressed people, hurled folk from their beds, and appeared in the form of a woman, a dog, or a billy goat. She drank a bottle of rosé wine vinegar at the burgomaster's home, yet the bottle was found full the next day.† She did quite a few other things.[4]

As everyone felt cremation of the body was the best solution, the body was exhumed and the coffin examined. It was observed that the cadaver was in the same state as Cuntze's had been before and *that it had devoured the grass of the turf* right down to the dirt. She was taken to the pyre with the customary ceremonies,‡ burned, then the remaining dirt was carefully scattered in some nearby running water, and thus came to an end the new hauntings of Bendschin and the individuals who had been crushed and squeezed rapidly recovered their health.

---

*Here is a new theme—that of order: the dead woman wants the living to observe a cleanliness code.

†A detail borrowed from the descent of fairies into houses on certain dates.

‡Those mentioned earlier with respect to Cuntze.

Notes

Introduction

1. Some of the narratives were published in Jacques Goimard and Roland Stragliati, *Histoire des morts-vivants* (Paris: France Loisirs, 1978); D. Sturm and K. Völker, *La Grande Anthologie du fantastique, Von denen Vampiren oder Menschensaugern* (Munich: Suhrkamp, 1994), Phantastische Bibliothek, st 2281. We may also refer to the studies by Gerda Knödl, *Der Vampir in der Literatur des 20. Jahrhunderts,* 1994; Carol A. Senf, *The Vampire in Nineteenth Century English Literature* (Bowling Green, Ohio: Bowling Green State University Popular Press, 1988); W. Lottes, "Dracula and Co. Der Vampir in der englischen Literaturen," *Archiv für das Studium der neueren Sprachen und Literaturen* 220 (1983), 285–99; Ronald Hochhausen, *Der aufgehobene Tod im französischen Populärroman des 19. Jahrhunderts: Ewiger Jude, Vampire, Lebenselixire* (Heidelberg: Carl Winter Verlag, Studia Romanica, 1988), 71.

2. K. M. Schmidt, "Dracula, der Herrscher der Finsternis," in U. Müller and W. Wunderlich, *Mittelater Mythen 2: Dämonen, Monster, Fabelwesen* (Saint-Gall: UVK Fachverlag für Wissenschaft und Studium, 1999), 185–204, page 185 here.

3. Margit Dorn, *Vampirfilme und ihre sozialen Funktionen* (Frankfurt: Peter Lang), 1994.

4. Voltaire, *Oeuvres complètes* [Complete Works], volume 20 (Paris: Garnier, 1879), 550.

5. Schmidt, "Dracula, der Herrscher der Finsternis," 196.

6. W. Schemme, "Die Braut von Korynth: von der literarischen Dignität des Vampirs," *Wirkendes Wort* 36 (1986), 335–46.

7. L. Gozlan, "Le Vampire de Val-de-Grâce," in *La Presse* (June 12–July 17, 1861).

8. Paul Féval, *Les drames de la mort. 1 La chambre des amours; 2. La Vampire* (Paris: Librairie Hachette, 1865), 241.

9. Paul Féval, *La Ville vampire, aventure incroyable de Mme Anne Radcliffe* (Paris: Dentu, 1875), 250.

10. "Les sources régionales de la Savoie" under the direction of J. Cuisenier (Paris: n.p., 1879), 613.

11. Montague Summers, *The Vampire, His Kith and Kin* (New York: University Press, 1960).

Chapter 1. The Vampire Myth

1. Appeared as a serial in the newspaper *La Presse,* June 12–July 7, 1861.

2. My quotes are borrowed from G. Camille's translation that appeared in the *Histoire des fantômes anglais* [History of English Ghosts] by Edmond Jaloux (Paris: Gallimard, 1962), 23–92. [The quotes are cited from the English original in this translation. —*Trans.*]

3. G. Schief and P. Viotto, *Tout l'oeuvre peint de Füssli* (Paris: Flammarion, 1980), plate 17. See also B. Terramorsi, "La Revenance du *Nightmare* de Heinrich Füssli dans la littérature fantastique," in J. Bessière and F. Montaclair, eds. *La Littérature comparée et les arts: les motifs du fantastique* (Paris: Ellipses, 1998).

4. Bram Stoker, *Dracula* (New York: W. W. Norton, 1996).

5. R. Howletts, ed., *Historia rerum Anglicarum* V, 24, in *Chronicles of the Reigns of Stephen, Henry II, and Richard I,* vol. 1 (London: Longman Rolls Series, 1884).

6. Text published in *Histoires des morts vivants* (Paris: n.p., 1977), 67–104; B. Terramorsi, "Une Cure d'amour: *La Morte Amoureuse* de Théophile Gautier," in *Bulletin de SFLGC* 13 (1992), 75–100.

7. Elizabeth Signorotti, "Repossessing the Body. Transgressive Desire in *Carmilla* and *Dracula,*" in *Criticism* 38, 607–32.

8. P. A. Ponson de Terrail, "La baronne trépassée," in *Le Moniteur du Soir* (March 25/May 29, 1852).

9. F. Paul Wilson, *The Keep* (New York: William Morrow and Co., 1981).

10. Julia Kristeva, *Pouvoirs de l'horreur* (Paris: Seuil, 1980), 12.

11. Complete text can be found in Claude Lecouteux, Philippe Marcq, *Les Esprits et les Morts* (Paris: Honore Champion, 2000), 113.

12. Claude Lecouteux, "Zur Vermittlung mittelalterlichen Denkens und Wissens: Die Glossare ind Lexika als paraliterarischer Weg," in *Chloe* 16 (1993), 19–35.

13. Voltaire, *Philosophical Dictionary* (New York: E. R. Dumont, 1901).

14. Collin de Plancy, *Dictionnaire infernal* (Geneva: Slatkine, 1980), 676–83.

15. C. Augé, ed., *Nouveau Larousse illustré. Dictionnaire universal encyclopédique,* 8 vols. (Paris: Libraire Larousse, ca. 1901), vol. 7, col. 1216 a.

Chapter 2. Man, Life, Death

1. Censorinus, *De die natali,* G. Rocca-Serra, ed. and trans. (Paris: Vrin, 1980), 14, 7.

2. A. van Gennep, *Rites of Passage* (Chicago: University of Chicago Press, 1960).

3. J. C. Schmidt, "Le Suicide au Moyen Âge," *Annales* ESC 31 (1976), 3–28.

4. N. Belmont, *Les signes de la naissance* (Paris: Gérard Monfort, 2000).

5. Claude Lecouteux, *Fantômes et Revenants au Moyen Âge* (Paris: Ed. Imago, 1986). [Translated into English as *The Return of the Dead* (Rochester, Vt.: Inner Traditions, 2009).]

6. Claude Lecouteux, *Chasses fantastiques et Cohortes de la nuit au Moyen Âge* (Paris: Ed. Imago, 1999).

7. Cited by Collin de Plancy, *Dictionnaire infernal,* 346.

8. M. Vovelle, *La Mort et l'Occident de 1300 à nos jours* (Paris: Gallimard, 1983).

9. H. de Briel, *Le Roman de Merlin l'Enchanteur* (Paris: Klincksiek, 1971), 99.

10. Pierre de Cluny, *De miraculis* I, 23, ed. by D. Bouthillier, Turnhout, 1988 (CC, *Continuatio mediaevalis,* 83).

11. M. Lauwers, "Le Sépulcre des pères et les ancêtres. Note sur le culte des défunts à l'âge seigneurial," in *Médiévales* 31 (1996), 67–68, page 73 here.

12. For more on this point, see F. Potonnier, "Après la mort, constat des archives," in D. Alexandre-Bidon and C. Treffort, *A réveiller les morts. La mort au quotidien dans l'Occident médiéval* (Lyon: n.p., 1993), 157–65, page 163 here.

13. Boris Rybakov, *Le Paganisme des anciens Slaves,* trans. L. Gruel-Appert (Paris: PUF, 1994), 152.

14. Lecouteux, *Fantômes et Revenants au Moyen Âge,* 65–69.

15. L. N. Vinagradova, "Les Croyances slaves concernant l'esprit-amant," in *Cahiers slaves* 1 (1997), 284.

16. Cited by Joseph Klapper, "Die schlesischen Geschichten von den schädigenden Toten," in *Mittheilungen der schlesischen Gesellschaft für Volkskunde* 11 (1909), 68.

17. F. S. Monschmidt, *Ministerium exorcistitum* (Oppau: n.p., 1738), 72.

18. Gábor Klaniczay, "Decline of witches and rise of vampires in 18th-century Habsburg monarchy," *Ethnologia Europea* 17 (1987), 165–80, page 167 here.

Chapter 3. The Life of the Dead

1. Marie Capdecomme, *La Vie des morts. Enquête sur les fantômes d'hier et d'aujourd'hui* (Paris: Éditions Imago, 1997).

2. Thomas of Cantimpré, *Bonum universale de apibus* II, 57, 20 (Douai, France: Georges Colvenor, 1627).

3. Walter Scott, *Letters on Demonology and Witchcraft* (London: John Murray, 1830), Letter V.

4. Emmanuel Le Roy Ladurie, *Montaillou, village occitan, de 1294 à 1324* (Paris: Gallimard, 1975), 595.

5. J. Klapper, *Erzählungen des Mittelalters* (Breslau: 1914), reprinted in Hildesheim and New York, 1978, 80 (gouge out the eyes); 153 (strangle).

6. Bibliothèque nationale, French manuscript 15219.

7. Dom Calmet, *Dissertation sur les revenants en corps, les excommuniés, les oupires ou vampires* (Grenoble: Jérôme Million, 1986), 96.

8. Tharsander, *Schauplatz vieler ungereimter Meynungen und Erzehlungen, Worauf die unter dem Titul Der magiae naturalis* (Berlin, Leipzig: Stück, 1736), vol. 1, 8.

9. Josef Müller, *Sagen aus Uri,* 3 vols. (Basel: Urs Graf, 1929–1945), nos. 997, 998, 1059.

10. L. N. Vinagradova, "Les Croyances slaves concernant l'esprit-amant," in *Cahiers slaves* 1 (1997), 237–54.

11. Gervaise of Tilbury, *Otia imperialia,* III, 99.

12. Cesarius of Heisterbach, *Dialogus miraculorum atque magnum visionum* XII, 15, J. Stange, ed. (Bonn: n.p., 1851).

13. For more on all this, see Lecouteux, Marcq, *Les Esprits et les Morts,* 131.

14. "Die toten reiten schnell," in Bürger's work. This poet was inspired by a legend reported by Grässe, *Sagenbuch des preussichen Staates,* 2 vols. (Glogau: 1871), vol. 2, 1046; reprinted in Hildesheim and New York, 1977. The original text can be found in the appendix documentation.

15. J. C. Polet, ed., *European Literary Heritage,* vol. 4a (Brussels: DeBoeck, 1993); *Le Moyen Âge, de l'Oural à l'Atlantique, littératures d'Europe orientale* (Brussels: DeBoeck, 1993), 289–92.

16. Lecouteux, *Fantômes et Revenants au Moyen Âge.*

17. Grässe, *Sagenbuch des preussichen Staates,* 2.

18. Goethe, *Poems and Ballads of Goethe,* trans. W. E. Aytoun and T. Martin (London: W. Blackwood and Sons, 1859), 65–67.

19. *Schlesisches Labyrinth* (Breslau and Leipzig, 1737), 363–93; reprinted by J. G. T. Grässe, *Sagenbuch des preussichen Staates,* vol. 2, 214.

20. M. Jonval, *Les chansons mythologiques lettones* (Paris: Picard, 1929), nos. 1163, 1164, 1170.

21. Raymond McNally and Radu Florescu, *In Search of Dracula: A True History of Dracula and Vampire Legends* (New York: Warner Books), 1973, 121. Translated into French as *A la Recherche de Dracula* (Paris: Robert Laffont), 1973.

22. Claude Lecouteux, *Fées, Sorcières et Loup-Garous au Moyen Âge: histoire du double au Moyen Âge* (Paris: Éditions Imago, 1992), 59–78. [Translated into English by Clare Frock as *Witches, Werewolves and Fairies: Shapeshifting and Astral Doubles* (Rochester, Vt.: Inner Traditions, 2003).]

23. Martin Wehrmann, *Pommersche Provinzial-Blätter für Stadt und Land,* 5 vols. (Treptow an der Rega: Anzeiger, 1820–1823), vol, 3, 421.

Chapter 4. Precursors of the Vampire

1. Lecouteux, *Fantômes et Revenants au Moyen Âge.*
2. Walter Map, *De Nugis Curialium* II, 27, ed. M. R. James (Oxford: Oxford University Press, 1914); *Anecdota Oxoniensa* 14.
3. Charles Ferdinand de Schertz, *Magia posthuma* (Olomouc: Rosenburg, 1706).
4. Calmet, *Dissertation sur les revenants en corps* (Paris: Éditions Imago, 1997), 139.
5. Capdecomme, *La Vie des morts. Enquête sur les fantômes d'hier et d'aujourd'hui* (Paris: Éditions Imago, 1997).
6. *Flóamanna Saga* [Saga of the People of Floí], F. Jonsson, ed. (Reykjavik: Stofnun Árna Magnússonar, 1932), Islenzk Fornrit, XII.
7. Régis Boyer, trans., *Contes populaires d'Islande* (Reykjavik: Stofnun Árna Magnússonar, 1983), 50–53.
8. Joseph Pitton Tournefort, *Voyage en Levant* (Amsterdam: Compagnie van Boekverkopers, 1718), vol. 1, 52.
9. Klapper, "Die schlesischen Geschichten von den schädigenden Toten," 88.
10. Dom Calmet, *Dissertation sur les apparitions d'esprits et sur les vampires et sur les revenants de Hongrie, de Moravie* (Grenoble: n.p., 1986).
11. Boris Rybakov, *Le Paganisme des anciens Slaves* (Paris: PUF, 1992), 17, 159.
12. Calmet, *Dissertation sur les apparitions d'esprits.*
13. Philostatus, *Life of Apollonius of Tyana,* IV, 25, trans. F. C. Conybeare (New York: Macmillan, 1912).
14. I would like to thank J. P. Sémon (Paris-Sorbonne), who procured this text for me and translated it with a philological analysis.
15. Lecouteux, *Chasses fantastiques et Cohortes de la nuit au Moyen Âge.*
16. Saxo Grammaticus, *Gesto Danorum* V, 162, A. Holder, ed. (Strasbourg: n.p., 1858). *Egils saga einhanda Asmundar beserkjabana,* G. Jónsson, ed., in *Fornaldar sögur nordurlanda* III (Reykjavik: n.p., 1924), 323–65, chapters 7, page 338 here.
17. *Erik the Red's Saga,* in *The Vinland Sagas,* Keneva Kunz, trans. (London: Penguin, 2008), 38.
18. Burchard of Worms, *Decretum* XIX, 5, 179, H. J. Schmitz, ed., in *Die Bussbücher,* 2 vols. (Düsseldorf: n.p., 1898), vol. 2, 448.
19. M. L. Le Bail, "Le Mort sur le vif," *Hésiode, Cahiers d'Ethnologie méditerranéenne* 2 (1994), 157–77, page 172 here.
20. M. Ranft, *De masticatione mortuorum in tumulis* (1728), trans. D. Sonnier, (Grenoble: Petite Collection ATOPIA, 2, 1995), 25–27.

21. E. Rohde, *Der griechische Roman* (Leipzig: Teubner, 1900), 45.

22. Hieronymus Cardan, *Magia seu mirabilium historiam de spectris* (1597), 56.

23. Claude Lecouteux, *Au-delà du merveilleux: des croyances au Moyen Âge* (Paris: Presses Universitaire de Paris-Sorbonne, 1992), 87–117.

24. K. Ranke, "Alp," in H. Bächtold-Stäubli, *Handwörterbuch des deutschen Aberglaubens,* 10 vols., 2nd ed. (Berlin: n.p., 1987), vol. 1, col. 281–305, column 293 here.

25. de Schertz, *Magia posthuma.*

26. *Schlesisches historisches Labyrinth* (Breslau and Leipzig: n.p., 1737), 351.

27. L. C. F. Garmann, *De miraculis mutuorum* (Dresden and Leipzig: n.p., 1660), I, 3: *De cadaveribus, porcorum mandentium instar, in cryptis feralibus sonantibus, vulgo schmatzende Tode;* Philippus Rohr, *Dissertatio historico-philosophica de masticatione mortuorum* (Leipzig: n.p., 1679).

28. Calmet, *Dissertation sur les apparitions d'esprits,* 88.

29. *Malleus maleficarum* I, 15, (Strasbourg: 1486–1487); facsimile edition, Hildesheim and New York, 1992. Translated into French by A. Danet as *Le Marteau des sorcières* [The Hammer of the Witches] (Paris: n.p., 1973), 271. Translated into English by Montague Summers (London: Pushkin Press, 1951).

30. Ovid, *Fastes* II, 553.

31. C. Aelurius, *Grassische Chronik* (Leipzig: n.p., 1625), 236.

32. Tischrede no. 6823, in *Luthers Werke* (Weimar: Verlag Hermann Böhlaus Nachfolger, 1921), vol. 6, 214.

33. Cited by J. Klapper, "Die schlesischen Geschichten," 85.

34. G. Rzaczynski, *Historia naturalis curiosa regni Poloniae* (Sandomir: n.p., 1721), 35.

35. Martin Kolbitz, "Chronicle of Frankenstein," *Monatsschrift von und für Schleisien* 1 (1829), 411.

Chapter 5. Names of the Vampire

1. W. Mannhardt, "Über Vampyrismus," *Zeitschrift für deutsche Mythologie* 4 (1859), 259–82; J. J. Hanush, "Die vampyre," 198–201; Heinrich von Wlislocki, "Quälgeister im Volksglauben der Rumänen," in *Am Ur-Quell* 6 (1896), 90–92.

2. O. F. Karl, *Danzinger Sagen* (Anhuth: n.p., 1843), 39.

3. A. S. Pushkin, *Slovar' jazyka* (Moscow: Skola Jazyki Russkoj, 1949), 193.

4. E. Karagiannis-Moser, *Le Bestiaire de la chanson populaire grecque moderne* [Bestiary of the modern Greek folk song] (Paris: PUF, 1997), 311. On the zombie, see L. Volta, "Horror nella cultura di massa. Dal mito allo zombi," in *Quaderni di Filologia Germanica* 2 (1982), 193–211.

5. Collin de Plancy, *Dictionnaire infernal,* 346.

6. For more on the strigoï, see F. Karlinger, E. Turczinski, *Rumänische Sagen und Sagen aus Rumänien* (Berlin: Erich Schmidt Verlag, 1982), Europäische Sagen XI, 45.

7. W.S.G.E., *Curieuse und sehr wunderbare Relation, von denen sich neuer Dingen in Servien erzeigenden Blutsaugern oder Vampyrs,* (n.l., n.p., 1732), 85; but J. C. Pohle and J. G. Hertel know exactly what is going on in their *De hominibus post morten sangsuisugis vulgo sic dictis Vampyren* (Leipzig: n.p., 1732).

8. *The Travels of Three English Gentlemen from Venice to Hamburg,* in *The Harleian Miscellany,* vol. 4 (London: M. Cooper, 1745).

9. Johann Heinrich Zopf, *Dissertatio de vampyris Serviensibus* (Duisberg: n.p. 1733).

Chapter 6. How Do We Protect Ourselves from Vampires?

1. In a 1454 manuscript conserved at the Wroclaw Library, the *Latalec,* one variety of revenant is called *incubus;* J. Klapper, "Die schlesischen Gesichten," 63.

2. Ibid., 75.

3. See the declaration made by a dead man in Apulieus (*Metamorphoses* 1, 30, Thomas Taylor, trans. (London: Robert Triphook, 1822): "When this most sagacious guardian, said he, of my body, diligently watched over me, old enchantresses, ardently longing after the spoil of my members, and on this account having frequently been in vain changed into other forms, when they found they could not deceive his sedulous attention; having at length thrown over him the dark mist of drowsiness, and buried him in profound sleep, they did not cease to call me by my name, till my infirm joints and cold members struggled, by sluggish endeavors, to obey the mandates of the magic art."

4. P. Geiger, "Leichenwache," in *Handwörterbuch . . .* vol. 5, cols. 1105–1113, column 1108 here.

5. *Sammlung von Natur- und Medizingeschichten* 9 (1919), 114.

6. *Schlesische Provinzial-Blätter* 31 (Breslau: n.p., 1801), 274.

7. I have borrowed the following information from Johann Georg Schmidt, *Die gestriegelte Rockenphilosphie oder aufrichtige Untersuchung derer von vielen super-klugen Weibern hochgehaltenen Aberglauben,* 6 works in two volumes (Chemnitz, 1718–1722), reprinted in Leipzig in 1988, and from J. Grimm, *Deutsche mythologie,* 3 volumes, (Darmstadt: 1965), vol. 3, nos. 397, 828, 830, 935, 1060.

8. M. Zender, *Atlas der deutschen Volkskunde,* Neue Folge: Erläuterungen, vol. 1, (Marbourg: n.p., 1959–1964), 233–80. See also G. Wiegelmann, "Der lebende Leichnam im Volksbrauch," in *Zeitschrift für Volkskunde* 62 (1966), 161–83.

9. *Schlesische Provinzial-Blätter* 34 (1801), 186. In Silesia, the chisel in the back is proof of witchcraft first, then vampirism of the person examined.

10. Claude Lecouteux, *Charmes, Conjurations et Bénédictions: lexiques et formules* (Paris: Honoré Champion, 1996), Essais 17, 37.

11. P. Geiger, "Leiche," in H. Bächtold-Stäubli, *Handwörterbuch des deutschen Aberglaubens,* 10 volumes, 2nd edition (Berlin: Walter De Gruyer, 1987), vol. 5, columns 1024–60, column 1055 here.

12. Ranft, *De masticatione mortuorum in tumulis,* 122.

13. For more on this entire development, see N. Kyll, "Die Bestattung der Toten mit dem Gesicht nach unten," in *Trierer Zeitschrift für Geschichte und Kunst des Trierer Landes* 27 (1964), 168–83.

14. A. Dierkens, "La Mort, les Funérailles et la Tombe de Pépin le Bref (768)," in *Médiévales* 31 (1996), 37–51, page 39 here.

15. D. Alexandre-Bidon and C. Treffort, *A réveiller les morts* (Lyon: Presses de l'Université de Lyon, 1993) 190.

16. Translation of the complete text by C. Lecouteux and P. Marcq in *Les Esprits et les Morts,* 190–201.

17. J. Olrik and H. Raeder, *Gesta Danorum* I, 7 (Copenhagen: Levin and Munksgaard, 1931). This passage was used again by Olaus Magnus in his *Historia de gentis septrionalibus* in the sixteenth century.

Chapter 7. Identifying and Killing the Vampire

1. Quoted by Collin de Plancy, *Dictionnaire infernal,* 679.

2. Johann Friedrich Weitenkampf, *Gedanken über wichtige Wahrheiten aus der Vernunft und Religion* (Brunswick: n.p., 1754).

3. J. C. Harenberg, *Vernünftige und Christliche Gedancken über die Vampire oder Blautsaugende Toten* (Wolfenbüttel: n.p., 1733).

4. "Dracula, un enragé?" *Pour la Science,* November 1988, review of an article published in the journal *Neurology* written by Juan Gomez-Alonso, neurologist of Xeral Hospital in Vigo.

5. Klapper, "Die schlesischen Geschichten," 83.

6. *Bunzlauer Monatsschrift* (n.l., n.p., 1779), 297.

7. Calmet, *Dissertation sur les apparitions d'esprits,* 92.

8. Munich, National Museum of Bavaria, Inventory number 2623, painting 22/271, ca. 1510.

9. Mannhardt, "Uber Vampyrismus," 265; Ranft, *De masticatione mortuorum in tumulis,* 121.

10. Ranft, *De masticatione mortuorum in tumulis,* 103; W.S.G.E., *Curieuse und sehr wunderbare Relation,* 6.

11. William of Newbury, *Historia rerum Anglicarum,* V, 24, R. Howlett, ed., in *Chronicles of the Reign of Stephen, Henry II, and Richard I,* vol.1 (London: Jacob Tonson and R. Knaplock, 1884), 479–82. Complete translation of the text with commentary appears in Lecouteux and Marcq, *Les Esprits et les Morts,* 179–83.

12. Agnes Murgoci, "The Vampire in Romania," in *Folklore* 37 (1926), 326.

13. Ibid.

14. Cited by D. Sturm and K. Volker, *Von denen Vampiren oder Menschensaugern,* (Munich: Suhrkamp, 1994), 513.

15. Jean Markale, *L'Énigme des vampires* (Paris: Pygmalion, 1991), 55.

16. Cited by Klapper, "Die schlesischen Geschichten," 80.

17. Cited by D. Harmening, *Der Anfang von Dracula. Zur Geschichte von Geschichten* (Würzburg: Königshausen and Neumann, 1983), 63.

18. [Lecouteux, *The Return of the Dead* (Rochester, Vt.: Inner Traditions, 2009). —*Editor*]

19. Lecouteux, *Fantômes et Revenants au Moyen Âge,* 98–102.

20. Cited by J. Klapper, "Die schlesischen Geschichten."

21. Karin Lambrecht, *Hexenverfolgung und Zaubereiprozesse in den schlesischen Territorien* (Cologne: Böhlau, 1995), 398.

22. Cited by Calmet, *Dissertation sur les apparitions d'esprits,* 76.

23. Ibid., 69.

24. Ernest Jones, *On the Nightmare* (London: Hogarth Press, 1931).

25. René Girard, *Le Bouc émissaire* (Paris: Grasset, 1966).

26. Ibid., 93.

27. W. A. J. von Tettau and J. D. H. Temme, *Die Volkssagen Ostpreussens Litthauens und Westpreussens* (Berlin: n.p., 1837). Reprint in Hildesheim and New York, 1994, 275.

28. Calmet, *Dissertation sur les apparitions d'esprits,* 28.

29. Ibid., 284

Chapter 8. Questions and Answers

1. Christine Michoux, "Magie, dent et vampirisme," in *Frénesies* 3 (1987), 208. This blasphemous dimension finds its full strength in Coppola's film.

2. P. Ariès, *L'Homme devant la mort* (Paris: Editions du Seuil, 1977), 348.

3. Gábor Klaniczay, "Decline of witches and rise of vampires in 18th-century Hapsburg Monarchy," *Ethnologia Europaea* 17 (1987), 165–80; Karin Lambrecht, *Hexenverfolgung und Zaubereiprozesse in den schlesischen Territorien.*

4. Eva Pócs, *Between the Living and the Dead. A Perspective on Witches and Seers in the Early Modern Age* (Budapest: Central European University Press, 1997),

42; on the kinship of vampires, witches, werewolves, and nightmares: 79, 119, 142, 163.

5. Lambrecht, *Hexenverfolgung und Zaubereiprozesse in den schlesischen Territorien,* 392.

6. R. Delorme, *Les Vampires humains* (Paris: Albin Michel, 1978).

7. William of Newbury, *Historia rerum Anglicarum,* V, 24.

8. Cited by Dom Calmet, *Dissertation sur les apparitions d'esprits,* 141.

9. W.S.G.E., *Curieuse und sehr wundebare Relation,* 64.

10. M. Ranft, *De masticatione mortuorum in tumulis,* 33.

11. Ibid.

12. Lambrecht, *Hexenverfolgung und Zaubereiprozesse in den schleisischen Territorien,* 394.

13. Ranft, *De masticatione mortuorum in tumulis,* 120.

14. Ibid., 114.

15. Ibid., 112.

16. Ibid., 71.

17. Ibid., 84.

18. Ibid., 86.

19. Ibid., 115.

20. C. F. Garmann, *De miraculis mortuorum* (Dresden and Leipzig: n.p., 1660). Reprinted in Dresden in 1709.

21. J. Klapper, "Die schlesischen Geschichten," 86.

22. Weitenkampf, *Gedanken über wichtige Wahrheiten aus der Vernunft und Religion* (Brunswick: n.p., 1754).

23. N. Kyll, "Die Besttattung der Toten mit dem Gesicht nach unten," 180.

24. *La Mandragore* 3 (1998), 129.

25. L. Illis, "On Porphyria and the Aetiology of Werewolves," in *Proceeding of the Royal Society of Medicine* 57 (1964), 23–26.

26. "Dracula, un enragé?" in *Pour la Science.*

27. L. Kayton, "Relationship of the Vampire Legend to Schizophrenia," in *Journal of Youth and Adolescence* (1972).

28. For more detail, see Lecouteux, *Witches, Fairies, and Werewolves,* 178; and "Une singulière conception de l'âme: remarques sur l'arrière-plan de quelques traditions populaires," *Medieval Folklore* 2 (1992), 21–47.

29. Eva Pócs, *Between the Living and the Dead. A Perspective on Witches and Seers in the Early Modern Age* (Budapest: n.p., 1997), 31–34. On the double, see 36–44.

30. Edgar Morin, *L'Homme et la Mort* (Paris: Seuil, 1976), 156.

31. For the complete development of this point, see Lecouteux, *Witches, Fairies, and Werewolves.*

32. V. Meyer-Matheis, *Die Vorstellung eines alter ego in Volkerzählungen* (Diss. Freiburg-im-Breisgau), 1974.

Appendix 1. The Vampires of Medvegia

1. Reproduced by Calmet, *Dissertation sur les apparitions d'esprits,* 143–49.
2. *Visum & repertum. Über die so genannten Vampirs, oder Blut-Aussauger. So zu Medvegia in Servien, an der Türkischen Granitz, den 7 Januarii 1732. Geschehen. Nebst einem Anhang/von dem Kauen und Schmatzen der Todten in Gräbern* (Nuremberg: n.p., 1732).
3. Text from D. Storm, K. Völker, *Von denen Vampiren* (Frankfurt: Fischer Taschenbuch-Verl, 1994), 456–60.

Appendix 2. The Dead Woman's Shroud

1. Selt, *Sagen aux Breslau's Vorzeit* (Breslau: n.p., 1833), 50.

Appendix 3. The Vampire of Bendschin or Pentsch

1. This text was printed in the *Schlesisches Labyrinth* (Breslau and Leipzig: n.p., 1737), 363–93. For more on its transmission, see Klapper, "Die schlesischen Geschichten," 76; [An English language account of this was provided by Dr. Henry More in his *Antidote Against Atheism* (1653), which is not as detailed as the Weinreich text. Montague Summers reprinted the More text in his book *The Vampire in Europe* (London: Kegan, Paul, Trench, and Trubner, 1929). —*Trans.*].
2. Claude Lecouteux, "Ces bruits de l'au-delà," in *Revue des langues romanes* 101 (1997), 113–24.
3. *Liber differentiarum,* Migne, *Pat. Lat.* 83, column 53.
4. Lecouteux, *Au-delà du merveilleux,* 168–75.

Bibliography

Reference Works

Bunson, Matthew. *The Vampire Encyclopedia*. New York: Random House (Grammercy), 2001.

Carter, Margaret L. *The Vampire in Literature: A Critical Bibliography*. Ann Arbor: University of Michigan Press, 1989.

Cohen, Daniel. *Encyclopedia of Ghosts*. New York: Avon, 1991.

Curran, Bob. *Vampires: A Field Guide to Creatures that Stalk the Night*. Franklin Lakes, N.J.: Career Press, 2005.

Jänsch, Erwin. *Vampir-Lexicon. Die Autoren des Schrechens ind ihre blutsaugerischen Kreaturen. 200 Jahre Vampire in der Literatur*. Munich: Knaur, 2000.

Martin, Ricardo. *Vampires Unearthed: The Complete Multi-media Vampire and Dracula Bibliography*. New York: Garland, 1983.

Studies

Agazzi, Renato. *Il Mito del vampiro en Europa*. Poggibonsi: Antonio Lalli Editore, 1979.

Alexandre-Bidon, Daniéle, and Cécile Treffort. *A réveiller les morts. La mort au quotidian dans l'Occident medieval*. Lyon: Presses de l'Université de Lyon, 1993.

Angenot, Marc. *Le Roman populaire. Recherches en paralittérature*. Montréal: Presses de l'Université de Québec, 1975.

———. "L'au-delà des astronomes, des philosophes, des religieux." *Sciences et Avenir* (1998).

Barber, Paul. *Vampires, Burials, and Death: Folklore and Reality*. New Haven: Yale University Press, 1988.

Baudrand, Hélène. *Les Dents de la mort: le mythe des vampires, des origines au Dracula de F. F. Coppola*. Grenoble: IEP dissertation, 1993.

Boehlich, Ernst. "Die Bexe von Lewin (1345). Ein Beitrag zur Geschichte des Vampirisimus." *Glazer Heimatblätter* 14 (1928).

Buican, Denis. *Les Métamorphoses de Dracula: L'histoire et la légende.* Paris: Le Félin, 1993.

Burkhart, Dagmar. *Vampirglaube und Vampirsage auf dem Balkan.* Munich: n.p., 1966.

Cajkanovoc, Veselin. "The Killing of a Vampire." In *Folklore* 7/4 (1974).

Calmet, Dom Augustin. *Dissertation sur les apparitions d'esprits et sur les vampires et sur les revenants de Hongrie, de Moravie, etc.* Einseidln: n.p., 1749. Reprint Grenoble: Éditions Jérôme Million, 1986.

Capdecomme, Marie. *La Vie des morts. Enquête sur les fantômes d'hier et d'aujourd'hui.* Paris: Éditions Imago, 1997.

Copper, Basil. *The Vampire in Legend, Fact, and Art.* London: Corgi, 1975.

Corradi, Carla. *Vampiri europei e vampiri dell'area scimanica.* Messina: Rubbettino, 1995.

Cremene, Adrien. *Mythologie du vampire en Roumanie.* Monaco: Rocher, 1981.

Davanzati, Guiseppe. *Dissertatione sopra I vampiri.* Naples: n.p. 1789.

Delorme, Roger. *Les Vampires humains.* Paris: Albin Michel, 1978.

D'Elvert, Christian. "Die Vampyre in Mähren." In *Schriften der historisch-statistischen Section der k.k. mährisch-schlesischen Gesellschaft* 12 (1859).

Dorn, Margit. *Vampirfilme und ihre sozialen Funktionen. Ein Beitrag zur Genregeschichte.* Frankfurt: Peter Lang, 1994.

Faivre, Antoine. *Les Vampires. Essai historique, critique et littéraire.* Paris: Le Terrain Vague, 1962.

Fritschius, Johann Christian. "Eines Weimarischen Medici Mutmassliche Gedanken Von denen Vampyren." In *Oder sogenannten Blut-Saugern, Welchen zuletzt Das Gutachen Der Königl. Preussischen Societät derer Wissenschafften, Von gedachten Vampyren, Mit beygefüget ist.* Leipzig: n.p., 1732.

Geiger, P. "Leiche." Cited in H. Bächtold-Stäubli. *Handwörterbuch des deutschen Aberglaubens,* 10 volumes, 2nd edition. Berlin: Walter De Gruyter, 1987, vol. 5, cols. 1024–60.

———. "Leichenwache." Vol. 5, cols. 1105–13.

———. "Nachzehrer." Vol. 6, cols. 812–23.

———. "Unverwest." Vol. 8, cols. 1496–97.

Grober-Glück, Gerda. "Aufhocker und Aufhocken." In Matthias Zender. *Atlas der deutschen Volkskunde.* Erläuterungen zur 4. Lieferung, Marbourg: Elwert Verlag, 1966.

———. "Der Vorstorbene als Nachzehrer." In Matthias Zender. *Atlas der deutschen Volkskunde.* Erläuterungen zu den Karten 43–48, Marbourg: Elwert Verlag, 1981. *Harenberg, Johann Christoph. Vernünfrige und Christliche Gedancken über die Vampire oder Blautsaugende Toten.* Wolfenbüttel: n.p., 1733.

Harmening, Dieter. *Der Anfang von Dracula. Zur Geschichte von Geschichten.* Würzburg: Königshausen and Neumann, 1983 (Quellen & Forschungen zur europäischen Ethnologie, 1).

Hochhausen, Ronald. *Der aufgehobene Tod im französischen Populärroman des 19. Jahrhunderts: Ewiger Jude, Vampire, Lebenselixire.* Heidelberg: Carl Winter Verlag, 1988 (Studia Romanica, 71).

Hock, Stefan. *Die Vampyrsagen und ihre Verwertung in der deutschen Literatur.* Berlin: n.p., 1900.

Jaworskij, Juljan. „Sudrüssische Vampire." In *Zeitschrift des Vereins für Volkskunde* 8 (1898).

Jones, Ernest. *On the Nightmare.* London: Hogarth Press, 1931.

Klapper, Joseph. "Die schlesischen Geschichten von den schädigenden Toten." *Mittheilungen der schlesischen Gesellschaft für Volkskunde* 11 (1909).

Kyll, Nikolaus. "Die Bestattung der Toten mit dem Gesicht nach unten." *Trierer Zeitschrift für Geschichte und Kunst des Trierer Landes* 27 (1964).

Lambrecht, Karin. *Hexenverfolgung und Zaubereiprozesse in den schlesischen Territorien.* Cologne: Böhlau, 1995 (Neue Forschungen zur schlesischen Geschichte, 4).

Lecouteux, Claude. *Chasses Fantastiques et Cohortes de la nuit au Moyen Âge.* Paris: Éditions Imago, 1999.

———. *The Return of the Dead: Ghosts, Ancestors, and the Transparent Veil of the Pagan Mind.* Rochester, Vt.: Inner Traditions, 2009.

———. *Witches, Werewolves, and Fairies: Shapeshifters and Astral Doubles in the Middle Ages.* Rochester, Vt.: Inner Traditions, 2003.

———. "Les Âmes errantes." *Sciences et Avenir* 117 (1998).

———. "Un singulière conception de l'âme: remarques sur l'arrière-plan de quelques traditions populaires." *Medieval Folklore* 2 (1992).

Le Roy Ladurie, Emmanuel. *Montaillou, village occitan, de 1294 à 1324.* Paris: Gallimard, 1975.

Lottes, W. "Dracula & Co. Der Vampir in der englischen Literaturen." In *Archiv für das Studium der neueren Sprachen und Literatur,* 220 (1983).

McNally, Raymond and Radu Florescu. *In Search of Dracula: A True History of Dracula and Vampire Legends.* New York: Warner Books, 1973.

Mannhardt, W. "Über Vampyrismus." In *Zeitschrift für deutsche Mythologie* 4 (1859).

Marigny, Jean, ed., *Les Vampires. Colloque sur le vampirisme dans la légende, la literature et les arts.* Paris: Cahiers de l'Hermétisme, 1993.

Markale, Jean. *L'Énigme des vampires.* Paris: Pygmalion, 1991.

Masters, Anthony. *The Natural History of the Vampire.* London: Rupert Hart-Davis, 1972.

Metzger, E. "La mutilation des morts." *Mélanges Charles Andler.* Strasbourg: Istra, 1924.

Michoux, Christine. "Magie, dent et vampirisme." In *Frénésies* 3 (1987).

Morin, Edgar. *L'Homme et la Mort.* Paris: Seuil, 1976.

Müller, Ingeborg, and Lutz Röhricht. "Der Tod und die Toten." In *Deutsches Jahrbuch für Volkskunde* 13 (1967).

Murgoci, Agnes. "The Vampire in Romania." *Folklore* 37 (1926).

Nandris, Grigoire. *The Dracula Theme in the European Literature of the West and of the East.* New York: n.p., 1965.

Paban, Gabrielle de. *Histoire des fantômes et des démons.* Paris: Locard et Davi, 1819.

Plancy, Collin de. *Dictionnaire infernal.* Paris: Plon, 1850.

———. *Histoire des vampires.* Paris: n.p., 1820.

Eva Pócs. *Between the Living and the Dead. A Perspective on Witches and Seers in the Early Modern Age.* Budapest: Central European University Press, 1997.

Pohl, Helga. "Die Gruselgeschichte, ein Beitrag zur Psychoanalyse von Horrorliteratur." In *Zeitschrift f. psychosomatische Medizin* 31 (1985).

Pohle, J. C., and J. G. Hertel. *De hominibus post morten sangsuisugis vulgo sic dictis Vampyren.* Leipzig: n.p., 1732.

Ranft, Michaël. *De masticatione mortuorum in tumulis.* Translated by D. Sonnier. Grenoble: Jérôme Millon, 1995.

Rohr, Philippus. *Dissertatio historico-philosophica de masticatione mortuorum.* Leipzig: n.p., 1679.

Schertz, Karl Ferdinand von. *Magia Posthuma.* Olomouc: n.p., 1706.

Stock, Johannes Christianus. *Dissertatio physica de cadaveribus sanguisugis. Von denen so genannten Vampyren oder Menschen-Säugern.* Jena: Horn, 1732.

Summers, Montague. *The Vampire: His Kith and Kin.* New York: University Press, 1960.

———. *The Vampire in Europe.* New York: University Press, 1961.

Terramorsi, Bernard. "La Revenance du *Nightmare* de Heinrich Füssli dans la littérature fantastique." In J. Bessière and F. Montaclair, eds. *La Littérature comparée et les arts: les motifs du fantastique.* Paris: Collection Littérature comparée, 1998.

———. "Une Cure d'amour: *La Morte Amoreuse* de Théophile Gautier." *Bulletin de SFLGC* 13 (1992).

Thallóczy, Lajos. "Beiträge zum Vampyr-Glauben der Serben." *Ethnologische Mitteilungen aus Ungarn* (1887).

Tharsander. *Schauplatz vieler ungereimter Meynungen und Erzehlungen, Worauf die unter dem Titul Der magiae naturalis.* Berlin, Leipzig: Stück, 1736.

————. *Visum & repertum. Über die so genannten Vampirs, oder Blut-Aussauger. So zu Medvegia in Servien, an der Türkischen Granitz, den 7 Januarii 1732. Geschehen. Nebst einem Anhang/von dem Kauen und Schmatzen der Todten in Gräbern.* Nuremberg: n.p., 1732.

Wiegelmann, G. "Der lebende Leichnam im Volksbrauch." *Zeitschrift für Volkskunde* 62 (1966).

W. S. G. E. *Curieuse und sehr wundebare Relation, von denen sich neuer Dingen in Servien erzeigenden Blutsaugern oder Vampyrs.* N.l., n.p., 1732.

Wright, Dudley. *Vampires and Vampirism.* London: Rider, 1914.

Zopf, Johannes. *Dissertatio de vampyris Serviensibus.* Duisberg: n.p., 1733.

Anthologies, Novels, and Stories

Davies, David Stuart, ed. *Children of the Night* (*Wordsworth Mystery and Supernatural*). London: Wordsworth, 2007. (Includes Alexei Tolstoy's *The Family of the Vourdalak,* Le Fanu's *Carmilla,* and Polidori's *The Vampyre,* among others.)

Gautier, Théophile. *Clarimonde.* Translated by Lafcadio Hearn. New York: Brentano's, 1899.

————. *La Morte Amoureuse: Avatar et autres récits fantastiques.* Paris: Gallimard, 1981.

Hérold, A. F. *Les Contes du vampire.* Paris: n.p., 1891.

Lecouteux, Claude, and Philippe Marcq. *Les Esprits et les Morts.* Paris: Honoré Champion, 2000.

Ryan, Alan. *The Penguin Book of Vampire Stories.* London: Penguin, 1987. (This anthology provides an interesting selection of newer vampire stories as well as classics such as Polidori's work.)

Stoker, Bram. *Dracula.* New York: W. W. Norton, 1996.

Sturm, Dieter, and Klaus Völker. *Von denen Vampiren oder Menschensaugern.* Munich: Suhrkamp, 1994. (An excellent anthology with numerous extracts from eighteenth- and nineteenth-century documents.)

Vadim, Roger. *Histoires de vampires.* Paris: Robert Laffont, 1961.

Wheatley, Dennis, ed. *Uncanny Tales 1, Volume 9 of the Dennis Wheatley Library of the Occult.* London: Sphere, 1974. (This includes *Carmilla* and *Clarimonde* and the English translation of Gautier's *La Morte amoureuse.*)

Index